CONCILIUM

Theology in the Age of Renewal

CONCILIUM

Theology in the Age of Renewal

Volume 52: Liturgy

Prayer and Community

Edited by
Herman Schmidt

Herder and Herder

1970
HERDER AND HERDER
232 Madison Avenue, New York 10016

CONTENTS

Editorial   7

PART I

ARTICLES

Prayer in a Time of Doubt   11
MARK GIBBARD

The Many Forms of the One Prayer   26
JAN PETERS, O.C.D.

Are New Forms of Liturgical Singing and Music Developing?   37
JOSEPH GELINEAU, S.J.

The Bishop at Prayer in his Church   47
DENIS HURLEY, O.M.I.

The Bishop at Prayer in his Church   51
JAN VAN CAUWELAERT

The Priest Praying in the Midst of the Family of Man   56
GERARD BROCCOLO

Woman's Prayer and Man's Liturgy   73
ADRIANA ZARRI

Prayer in the Home—A Mother's Testimony   87
IANTHE PRATT

Home or Group Prayer and the Divine Office   92
DAVID POWER, O.M.I.

Table Prayers and Eucharist: Questions from the Social
Sciences   104
ROBERT LEDOGAR, C.F.M.S.

PART II
BULLETIN

Prayer and Song in the Human Family Today (Italy)   119
DOMENICO BILOTTI, S.J.

Prayer and Song in the Human Family Today (Ireland)   124
DIARMUID O'LAOGHAIRE, S.J.

A General View   128
HERMAN SCHMIDT, S.J.

PART III
DOCUMENTATION CONCILIUM

The Music and Language of Christian Worship

   i. The Language of Christian Worship   143
PLACID MURRAY, O.S.B.

   ii. Contemporary Church Music   147
ERHARD QUACK

Biographical Notes   151

Editorial

NOBODY with a sense of history will be astonished at what is happening in the Roman liturgy. When it developed its own rite between the fourth and seventh centuries, the consequent upheaval was not dissimilar from what we are experiencing today. In 1928 Abbot Cabrol, the well-known liturgiologist, spoke of the "liturgical revolution" of the fourth century.[1] This expression was taken over by Bourque in the standard work on the Roman Sacramentaries: "A radical change, a veritable liturgical revolution, took place in the West. Every Mass of the *Temporale* and the *Sanctorale* henceforward had its own formulary. This left the door wide open to authors anxious to exercise their talents in the composition of liturgical texts. It would even have been astonishing if the first enthusiasm had not led some converts to exaggerate, and so provoke, complaints and restrictions."[2]

C. Vogel speaks in similar terms in his standard work on the sources of the liturgy, where one chapter has the title: "The Period of Oral and Written Improvisation—from the Early Stages to Gregory I (590–604)."[3] In his Preface he remarked:

"This volume appears only a few months after Vatican II's Constitution on the Liturgy (4 Dec. 1963) and the Instruction

[1] F. Cabrol, "La Messe dans la liturgie. VI. La révolution liturgique du IVe siècle", in *Dict. Théol. Cath.*, x, 2 (1928), cc. 1365–6.
[2] E. Bourque, *Etude sur les Sacramentaires Romains* (Città del Vaticano, 1948), vol. I, pp. 11–12.
[3] C. Vogel, *Introduction aux sources de l'histoire du culte chrétien au moyen-âge. Biblioteca degli Studi Medievali*, 1 (Spoleto, 1966), pp. 20–42.

concerning its application (26 Sept. 1964). Among other reforms, the Latin Church has just started its second linguistic revolution in worship. The break between the Latin formulary and those in other languages will soon be complete. . . . This Introduction may have some relevance for certain parts of the liturgy, perhaps till 1965. But after that it will doubtless be classed among the studies of 'liturgical antiquities'."

The liturgical "revolution" need not lead to panic. This second liturgical revolution is in a sense a repetition of what happened in the classical age of the Roman liturgy—though it has its own characteristics. Since Vatican II, the liturgy has been freeing itself from the principles that dominated it since the Council of Trent. After Trent, the Latin liturgical heritage was selected, fixed and made compulsory for the whole Church in books that were uniform throughout. This obsession with uniformity has now been shaken off; the emphasis is changing from "universal" to "local", and the liturgical community is becoming less clerical and more popular in structure. That there are tensions is only to be expected. Crises and conflicts can hardly be avoided where there is life.

In this issue, we want to give a phenomenological description of the life of prayer as we know it today, with an eye on the development of the liturgy. The "how" and "what" of the way men pray today, as it is or should be, will throw some light on what prayer is. Three main articles examine the signs of the times and the various linguistic and musical expressions of modern prayer. In a second section, the "how" and "what" of prayer is examined in concrete detail: two bishops explain how they pray in their Church; a priest describes his experience of sacerdotal prayer in a large town; a woman looks at a liturgy made by men, and a mother talks about praying with her children. The praying, eating and drinking together of ordinary people is linked up with the divine office and the Eucharist. The Bulletin will deal with the literature of modern prayer.

HERMAN SCHMIDT
DAVID POWER
HELMUT HUCKE

PART I
ARTICLES

Mark Gibbard

Prayer in a Time of Doubt

I. Praying while Doubting

THERE is plenty of evidence that many people now pray less than they used to do, or at least that they pray with a less firm faith; and these include some who hold responsible posts in the churches. This dilemma about prayer is clearly expressed in Michael Novak's *Belief and Unbelief*:

> There seem to be many men today—and their numbers constantly increase—who both believe and disbelieve, who are not agnostics, but who recognize in their hearts a divided allegiance. Through all their busy activities for the betterment of men, they keep an "open mind" regarding a power or an intelligence they do not dare to call "God".... Who can say, to his own or anyone's satisfaction, what it is thoroughly to believe? or thoroughly to disbelieve?[1]

How widespread this has become was apparent in the fourth Assembly of the World Council of Churches at Uppsala. The Assembly accepted a report on worship, which after granting that many still found joy and reality in traditional forms of worship, stated:

> We know how deeply the question of worship troubles many as a personal anxiety. Some Christians seek to maintain a rhythm of personal prayer, despite repeated lapses. Some are nostalgic for the reality of prayer, as the presence of God in

[1] M. Novak, *Belief and Unbelief* (London, 1966), p. 15.

prayer becomes less and less real to them. Most feel guilty about their lack of prayer. Some have almost given up the effort to pray.[2]

Those who encounter these difficulties in prayer need to grapple with the intellectual issues honestly and thoroughly; and for some this may take a long time. It is not my purpose here to deal with the philosophical and related problems. The only question with which this article is concerned is: *Does such individuals' intellectual integrity compel them to give up any kind of praying, until they are much more clear about God?* I do not think so. There are two practical points. First, there is perhaps something in the inquirer's meeting with and serving other people, which is already a kind of praying, even though he may not yet see it in this light. Secondly, there may be a way of reflecting on and exploring life, a kind of meditation, which he might be able to use without loss of intellectual integrity; and this way of reflection may gradually merge into some of the more usual forms of prayer, as the colours of the spectrum merge into one another. These two practical suggestions would seem more reasonable if our normal idea of prayer could be widened.

II. A WIDER CONCEPT OF PRAYER

Our concept of prayer has been narrow, because our concept of God has been inadequate. Prayer has often been regarded as words, thoughts and desires addressed to God, a someone in the beyond, a third entity besides the world and themselves; and has been so because popular teaching has so over-stressed the transcendence of God as almost to neglect his immanence. But now many theologians are recalling us to a more balanced understanding of the being of God. They find themselves impelled to do this as they try to relate Christian faith to Western thought today, for example, to existentialism, empiricism and process-philosophy.[3] These theologians remind us that in various ways

---

[2] *Uppsala '68 Speaks* (Geneva, 1968), p. 78.
[3] See, for example, John Macquarrie, *Studies in Christian Existentialism* (London, 1966) and *God-Talk* (London, 1967); Norman W. Pittenger, *Process Thought and Christian Faith* (London, 1969); Ian Ramsey, *Religious Language* (London, 1957), which faces the issue of empiricism. Teilhard de Chardin has affinities with the process-philosophers.

God penetrates the whole universe, the course of history, and mankind in particular. The Logos in some measure lightens every man, whether he knows it or not. God in his dynamic immanence pervades all these areas, although we, in contrast to the pantheists, affirm that he is also the transcendent Lord over all. This balanced concept has always been found in orthodox theologians and mystical writers, but traditional theism has often tended to drift towards deism. These contemporary writers are doing valuable service for theology and for spirituality. Professor John Macquarrie has written:

> Criticisms of traditional theism are being met by the development of new forms of theism, and these in the long run will lead to a better and deeper understanding of Christian faith as a whole. Tillich, Hartshorne, Ogden, Herzog, Dewart—these are just a few names of men who, well aware of the inadequacies of traditional theism, are trying, in various ways and with varying degrees of success, to explicate the idea of God so that men today can know his reality.[4]

Indeed Hans Urs von Balthasar has gone so far as to say:

> The frightening phenomenon of modern atheism may, among other things, be a forcible measure of providence to bring back mankind, and especially Christendom, to a more adequate idea of God.[5]

This richer concept of God and greater stress on his living immanence can extend our understanding of prayer. Because God is not *a* being, not an entity, but is Being, who underlies and sustains the universe though he is not confined to it, prayer, which is encounter with the being of God, can be as wide as life. Meeting and serving others and also reflecting on and exploring into life can be prayer in this sense, for all these activities are a real encountering of God, though often incognito in his immanence. Some people go on in this way for a long time without being conscious of their encounter with God. But we may confidently hope that gradually or suddenly they will come to know that they

---

[4] John Macquarrie, *God and Secularity* (London, 1968), p. 109.
[5] H. U. von Balthasar, *The God Question and Modern Man* (New York, 1967), pp. 96–7.

have met with God as personal being or rather he has met with them: "You have come to know God or rather to be known by God" (Gal. 4. 9).

If anyone should think that such a widening of the concept of prayer is illegitimate, we may notice that St Paul himself widened in rather a similar way the concept of worship. In Romans 12. 1 he took the word *latreia*, commonly used for worship in the narrow sense of the cultus, and stretched it to cover the whole of our life: "I appeal to you therefore, brethren, by the mercies of God, to present your bodies as a living sacrifice, holy and acceptable to God, which is your reasonable worship" (*logiké latreía*). Then he devoted the rest of the chapter to explaining the width of this worship; *latreia* means, he said, the using of all our varied gifts energetically and corporately in the service of all men, friendly or hostile.

III. LABORARE EST ORARE

So perhaps we can give a new turn of meaning to the old saying *Laborare est orare*. Then we can use it to try to show those who are finding faith and conventional prayer difficult that meeting and working for others may be at least the beginning of prayer in this wider sense. The Uppsala report itself urges the Churches to use this approach to help men in doubt towards faith and prayer:

> We believe that in the service of their neighbour, men can meet the Lord, to whom the community of faith looks in prayer, that that community is open to and supports the perplexed, and that the desire to pray is the groping of doubt into faith.[6]

This is not a new idea; there are hints of it in the Bible. The book Ecclesiasticus said about the craftsmen of the city: "They keep stable the fabric of the world and their prayer is in the practice of their trade" (Ecclus. 38. 34). In a similar way Jeremiah spoke with approval about King Josiah: "He judged the cause of the poor and needy; then it was well. Is not this to know me? says the Lord" (Jer. 22. 16). It is to be noticed that the prophet did not say that judging the poor and needy was a result of

[6] *Uppsala '68 Speaks* (Geneva, 1968), p. 78.

knowing God through prayer, but rather that judging the poor and needy was in itself a knowing of the Lord. Further, there is the saying in the gospel, "I was in prison and you came to me" (Matt. 25. 36). If to come to the Lord is the heart of prayer, then these words imply that this act of service was in itself a kind of prayer. So we have good reason to say that those who are doing altruistic service may in this wider sense be beginning to pray— without realizing it.

A necessary word of caution. Few things exasperate humanitarian agnostics or vague believers more than any implication that without knowing it they are in some way believers and men of prayer. Honesty demands that Christians should avoid what looks like acquisitive terminology. Yet although agnostics' service to their fellow men is certainly not prayer in their own sight, it may in the light of Christian faith be seen to be at least the beginning of prayer in this wider sense. But if meeting and serving of others are to become prayer with greater depth, two things are necessary; first, we need to realize increasingly the total needs of our neighbours; and secondly, the motives of our service need progressively to be purified from egoism.

Firstly, our service for others may begin with their need for food, shelter and medical care. Planned reform in education may be another need. This may necessitate political or social pressure on government authorities. Then these actions will be part of this wider prayer. A further need may be to help people to bring their personal relationships to a more satisfactory level. All these needs are apparent both to Christians and agnostics. Yet the effectiveness of Jesus' care and service of others was inseparably interwoven with his own sense of personal, direct dependence on God; and Christians would affirm that another need of human nature is this sense of fellowship with God analogous to our need for human fellowship. So the experience of trying to meet the complete needs of men and women may itself lead us eventually to the conviction succinctly expressed by Hans Urs von Balthasar: "The created person who is loved is grasped in his true reality only in relation to God."[7] In this way our service and prayer may deepen *pari passu*.

[7] H. U. von Balthasar, *op. cit.*, p. 147.

Secondly, the other condition necessary if serving others is to lead to more profound prayer is the gradual purification of our own motives from egoism. Helping others can easily be spoilt by paternalism and patronage. These failings are the almost inevitable outcome of the pride and self-centredness so subtly and deeply rooted in our human nature. Experience shows that we cannot eliminate these defects by ourselves. If, self-consciously and systematically, we attempt to do so by our own efforts, often all that happens is that we become proud that we are not quite so proud as we used to be. We are caught in a vicious circle of pride, from which we may perhaps escape only by some form of prayer and worship. In true worship we begin to lose our preoccupation with self and reputation, by looking away from self-concern and towards God who is all in all. Increasingly in this worship we desire simply to give ourselves to God so that he can use us as he wishes. If such worship is genuine and deep, this unself-conscious generosity is often carried over almost subconsciously into service and daily relationships. Yet we must admit that some who are most regular in formal worship are often self-complacent and self-centred, whereas some agnostics are admirably unself-conscious in their service. Yet there is considerable evidence to show that "if we would attempt to do good with any sure hope that it will prove good and not evil, we must act in the spirit of humility; and worship alone can make us humble".[8] Worship can remove egoism from our service.

IV. Reflection and Exploration

For those who are uncertain about God, there is another way into prayer in its wider sense. This is a kind of meditation, or reflection upon and exploration of the richness of life. We may confidently hope that in time this will lead many to personal encounter with God transcendent as well as immanent, and bring them to express to him their gratitude, desires and requests. But nowadays many have to begin with a straightforward, non-religious reflection on life, because to them traditional religious language is almost meaningless. To be of value, their reflection must start with what seems to them to be real and authentic. Hence

[8] K. E. Kirk, *Vision of God* (London, 1931), p. 449.

they cannot begin with God—or at least with God in the way many people have thought about him in the past. Initially, it is preferable if they reflect on their own experience; if this reflection is as sincere and as deep as is possible at the time, it can be prayer in its wider sense. Of course an agnostic would not wish to speak like this of his own reflections, yet, in the light of faith, believers can see the agnostic's reflections in this way, for, as von Balthasar says: "We have to recall that God, the sea and abyss of Being, is not a being among others, hence not an 'object' that might be detached from a surrounding world and especially not from the knowing subject."[9]

Nowadays, it is usually best to begin with reflections on experiences of wonder, joy, relief and gratitude rather than with those of need or weakness, particularly because, as Bonhoeffer said, many modern people suspect that religion is a "snuffing around in the sins of men in order to catch them out", and also because it is important to declare immediately that "we frankly recognize that the world and man have come of age, and that we do not speak ill of man in his worldliness but confront him with God at his strongest point".[10]

As a step towards reflecting on life with gratitude many people might be advised to express their gratitude spontaneously in daily life. At moments of thankfulness, of exhilaration and of achievement, they should exclaim "Thanks be to God," or even just "Thanks be", more or less spontaneously, even though they may be very vague about God. They should also express gratitude and relief to their friends more freely and spontaneously, while making allowance for different people's temperaments. Words of gratitude not only express but also deepen our sense of dependence on one another, and may eventually lead us to a sense of dependence on that great underlying reality, which believers call God. Dr Harry Guntrip, a psychiatrist, has said that this living sense of dependence is essential both for human maturity and for religious faith, so that they support one another.

[9] H. U. von Balthasar, *op. cit.*, p. 147.
[10] D. Bonhoeffer, *Letters and Papers from Prison* (London, 1965), pp. 117–18 (*Wiederstand und Ergebung. Briefe und Aufzeichnungen aus der Haft* [Munich, 1952], pp. 235–6).

Dependence is . . . an ineradicable element in human nature, and the whole development of love and affection arises out of our need for one another. From this point of view religion is concerned with the basic fact of personal relationship and man's quest for a radical solution to the problems that arise out of his dependent nature.[11]

Becoming open to one another may help us to become open to God.

Besides these spontaneous words of thankfulness there is need to set aside times for reflective gratitude. Then it is useful to try to find some kind of natural link between these experiences. Personal relationships are often deepened in this way when friends reflect with gratitude over earlier meetings and conversations. A similar inter-relating of our reflections may weave a kind of pattern of gratitude into our lives, deepen our confidence in life, and give us the desire and the courage to explore it.

These times can be even more valuable if they include appreciative reflection about other people, particularly about those whose abilities and achievements might make us envious or against whom we might harbour resentments. Such reflection might make us more realistic about ourselves and more free from jealousy and animosity; then our exploration of life would be more objective and discerning. We find this kind of reflective gratitude in the great men of faith and of prayer. Paul wrote to the Christians at Philippi: "I thank my God whenever I think of you" (Phil. 1. 3, NEB). He could even say of the Church at Corinth, though it was spoilt by rivalries and scandals: "I am always thanking God for you. I thank him for all the enrichment that has come to you in Christ" (1 Cor. 1. 4–5). He discerned and reflected on the signs of goodness behind the unattractive exterior of this Christian community. This thankfulness encouraged Paul to devote himself to their service; and in this setting he prayed for them. Gratitude, devotion to service, and prayer is a sequence that today may lead some people to intercession.

In our age reflective gratitude must include thankfulness for the benefits of science, medicine and technology. This part of re-

---

[11] H. Guntrip, quoted in E. James (ed.), *Spirituality for Today* (London, 1968), p. 33.

flective gratitude might also—indirectly—do something to remove the lurking groundless fear of some that science is inimical
to faith and prayer. But in this age of technology there is perhaps
a danger that some people may develop a dominative frame of
mind, because in their daily work they have, as it were, to stand
over nature and seize and apply its resources and energies for
purposes of development. But a dominative outlook, however ac-
quired, is good neither for personal relationships nor for the life
of faith and prayer. The grateful appreciation of literature and
poetry can have a counterbalancing effect.

In contrast to the technologist the lover of literature must sit
beneath the given text and let it speak to him. He needs to read,
not with a childish docility, but with an "informed docility" aris-
ing from his past experience and study. In the building up of
good personal relationships, this "informed docility" is clearly an
asset with its ability to draw on the past and its readiness to be
led forward into the future. Equally, it is an asset in the exploration of life, which is prayer. In this search many have
eventually realized that they have been met by one infinitely beyond them. The heart of what they have experienced may be in-
expressible, like some experiences of friendship and human love;
but if words can be employed at all, it is often in poetry or illu-
minative imagery that they speak most adequately. The Bible
contains so much of the experience of the pioneers of this search
(as well as evidence of the sluggish resistance of self-centred
human nature); and these scriptures are to a great extent a library
of poetry and allusive imagery, indeed far more so than the aver-
age Christian realizes. That is why Karl Rahner was justified in
writing: "The capacity and practice of perceiving the poetic word
is a presupposition of hearing the Word of God. . . . In its inmost
essence, the poetic is a prerequisite for Christianity."[12] Countless
people also need to express gratitude for art and music, which
have played a major part in their discovery of the wealth and
range of life and of its depths where God discloses himself. The
appreciation of the beauty and of the moods of nature and above
all the enrichment of life through companionship and love power-

[12] K. Rahner, s.j., "Poetry and Christian", in *Theological Investigations*
(London, 1966), IV, p. 363.

fully feed this reflective gratitude, and often lead towards communion with God at the heart of reality.

In stressing reflective gratitude, we cannot ignore the evils of
life, which will not fit into it.[13] We must not minimize these problems with superficial answers. True, there are unresolved
dilemmas in nearly all fields of reflection and study, but for believers this catalogue of evil is formidable indeed. These evils
stand like the geologists' erratic boulders, odd and not belonging
to the landscape. Reflective gratitude must neither make us blind
to them nor make us acquiesce in them, but rather strengthen us
to face their challenge and battle through them. This reflection
upon and exploration into life may lead us eventually to share
in the insight of St Paul: "In everything, as we know, he (the
Spirit) co-operates for good with those who love God and are
called according to his purpose" (Rom. 8. 28). Thus the apostle
faced the hard side of life and inspired others with courage.

If times of reflection are going to have this practical effect on
men's lives, how are these times best spent? Everyone must discover what is effective for himself and be ready for change. We
can learn from others, and it is less trouble to learn from their
mistakes than from our own. Many Christians begin their times
of reflection by realizing the presence of God. This does not mean
that they make some imaginative figure of God; but more often
that they reflect on some words of Scripture. They may think of
Jesus or of some significant action or words of his, because they
believe that in him there is a unique disclosure of God, the underlying reality of all things. On the other hand people who are uncertain about God presumably have comparable methods of concentrating their attention and then of choosing some perspective
for their reflection. Nearly everyone will find something helpful
in this description of meditative reflection by an American Roman
Catholic nun:

> The moment of prayer is necessary if one is to be fully and
> humanly present to one's fellow men when the time for such
> encounter arrives. Such meditative moments are a constant

[13] For the problem of evil, see John Hick, *Evil and the God of Love*
(London, 1966); Austin Farrer, *Love Almighty and Ills Unlimited* (London, 1962).

re-assessing of the value of human things . . . and a deepening of one's appreciation for the contacts with one's neighbour and with the world. . . . We need to stand back at times to get a broader view, lest our own little particular loves, our own secure little corners of the world blur our cosmic vision.[14]

These times can renew and refresh us in the pressure of life, though we must be careful lest they degenerate into day-dreaming. Many people discover for themselves the value of regular, if possible daily, reflection. Yet even the keenest miss occasionally their times through laziness or self-indulgence; yet they do not always fail through self-indulgence, but sometimes because prayerful reflection itself appears to be a form of self-indulgence, a misuse of time, and a substitute for a more urgent duty. But if meditative reflection is actually a reassessing of the situation, a deepening of your appreciation of others and a gathering of your forces, then its regular practice is normally time well spent. When it has to be omitted on days of abnormal pressure, the habitual perspective which it gives should carry people through such exceptional times.

V. THE FUNCTION OF AN ADVISER

Each individual must find his own way. No one must be dragooned. Yet a good adviser can save you a good deal of frustration. He can tell you what ways run into dead ends. But probably his two chief uses will be to guide your reading and to help you to deal with discouragements.

There is an immense literature in this area. But what will feed and give direction to your reflection? Our predecessors, men and women of most diverse types, have left us their own first-hand accounts, diaries, prayers and writings. These are generally more stimulating than rehashed descriptions of methods of meditation and prayer. But this material needs to be read with discrimination and personal adaptation, because the philosophical, religious and social outlooks represented are so different from our own; most of such works were written when the understanding of certain aspects of human nature was inevitably less profound than it is

[14] G. M. Schutte, S.Sp.S., "Reflections on Prayer and World Holiness", in *Worship* (Feb. 1967), p. 110.

today. Particularly valuable are writings which show a first-hand knowledge of the typical problems of modern man, such as Dag Hammarskjöld's *Markings* (London, 1964).[15]

A basic book in this search will be the Bible, but many modern people cannot accept it as an authoritative volume, since they see that it is a library of books of very varying value. Readers would be well advised to concentrate at first on those passages which nourish their own gratitude and trust, and—for a time at least— to leave the rest. Baron von Hügel, that encyclopaedic scholar and man of prayer, advised beginners to be like cows in the meadow —to feed on the particular grass that at the moment suited them, not to waste energy in snorting at the kind of grass they found inedible—and also to chew the cud.[16]

The second task of the adviser is to help us to fight our way through discouragement, which is probably the most serious obstacle to exploration through prayer. Often nothing seems to happen. It is like this in human companionship and love. There are high moments; there are uneventful and rather dull periods; and there may be times of seemingly dead unresponsiveness. By going on together through all these experiences human friends and lovers can deepen their relationships with one another; and so it is in this exploration of life which is prayer. Sometimes light dawns quite unexpectedly, even as in natural science;[17] it occurred to Archimedes, as he was stepping out of the bath, how to test whether the king's crown was of gold or of some alloy, and he rushed out naked shouting, "I have found it". So for those who persevere in the search of prayer, light comes suddenly or gradually like the dawning of a day. They may be led to a change of outlook on life, which the New Testament calls *metanoia*; and they may realize the need of a personal bond and commitment to God. These things happen in many different ways, and it is fortunate if there is an experienced guide at hand.

[15] Many have found the value of this book doubled by Henry P. van Dusen's *Dag Hammarskjöld, a biographical interpretation* (New York, 1966; London, 1967).

[16] F. von Hügel, *Selected Letters* (London, 1927), p. 268.

[17] For the place of discovery and illumination in natural science, see Professor M. Polanyi, *Personal Knowledge* (London, 1958).

VI. Corporate Seeking and Praying

Nowadays, in many places the small informal group is very effective in helping people to discover what prayer really is. This is not the traditional prayer-circle long familiar in many churches. It is a mixed group consisting partly of those with some experience of prayer and partly of inquirers and seekers. They need to come to know one another sufficiently well to share their convictions and experiences freely and humbly. They would not think of themselves as being divided into teachers and learners, for everyone seems to gain from this fellowship. Apparently, such a group produced *Prayers of Life*, one of the most unconventional and unpretentious of books, which in its many translations has stimulated a very wide variety of people.[18]

These groups promote openness and mutual trust. One of the common hindrances to growth in prayer is the lack of good interpersonal relationships. St Thomas Aquinas has a perceptive sentence in *Contra Gentiles*: "For a man to be open to divine things he needs tranquillity and peace; now mutual love, more than anything else, removes the obstacles to peace."[19] It is mutual love (*dilectio mutua*) which creates tranquillity of mind, which in turn is the prerequisite of truly waiting upon God (*vacare Deo*). This is what the first epistle of John says: "Everyone who loves is a child of God and knows God, but the unloving know nothing of God" (1 John 4. 7). Groups which come to this quality of mutual trust and love cannot be organized, but in many places today the human soil seems congenial to their growth.

Besides discussion, these groups often wish for periods of silence and prayer, which may be partly free prayer and partly in liturgical forms. There must never be any forcing of the pace. Each group has to discover for itself what kind of balance of prayer is suitable to it. In many places the *Office of Taizé*[20] or,

---

[18] M. Quoist, *Prayers of Life* (Dublin, 1961). (The original version was *Priéres*, 1954, published by Editions Ouvriéres, Paris.)

[19] *Ad hoc quod homo divinis vacet, indiget tranquillitate et pace. Ea vero quae pacem perturbare possunt, praecipue per dilectionem mutuam tolluntur* (St Thomas Aquinas, *Contr. Gent.* Book 3: ch. 117).

[20] *Office de Taizé* (Taizé, 1964), bound up with the Psalter from the *Bible de Jérusalem*, and with a supplement of the office of the Blessed Virgin Mary for the use of Catholics (Taizé Office: English translation, London, 1966).

more often, selected parts of it, has met the needs of such groups.
A more recent book from which suitable material might be chosen
is an ecumenical *Daily Office*[21] compiled by an official group of
Anglicans, Presbyterians, Methodists, Congregationalists and
Baptists, with a Roman Catholic observer. It provides a biblical
lectionary, short selections from the Psalms and canticles, and
outlines for thanksgiving and intercession in free prayer.

Some groups have discovered that a eucharist can be an excel-
lent setting for their discussion and fellowship. The eucharist in
its different forms has always been the place where men have reflected on what has been disclosed in Scripture about the purpose
of the world and of the Church; where they have shared together
in a meal; and where they have committed themselves in prayer
and service for the world. A eucharist in someone's house or in a
students' group can be more flexible and less stylized than in a
parish church. It is surprising how such a eucharist can speak to
and help those who are full of doubts. In a paper to former members of his seminary, a theological student explained what the
college eucharist meant to him, even in his most perplexed
moments:

> The world picture which I then had was one into which the
> notion of a transcendent God just did not fit. . . . This approach
> made nonsense of prayer and worship, traditionally understood.
> Any idea of praying to someone, of talking to someone, of try-
> ing to bring one's will into line with God's will was nonsensi-
> cal. . . . But the *one* service which did make sense was the
> eucharist, in terms of the gathering of the whole local accept-
> ing community round the re-presentation of the self-giving
> Christ. Gathered together in this context, the Church is empow-
> ered to love and to accept.[22]

In its new provisional liturgy the Church of England has provided a text suitable as a basis for such eucharists; it has a clear

[21] *Daily Office* by a Joint Liturgical Group, edited by Ronald C. D. Jasper
(London, 1969).
[22] *Fresh Springs*, No. 3, 1965; an occasional paper of Lincoln Theological
College, England.

structure, it is flexible, and it allows for free prayer as well as set forms.[23]

Unfortunately, perhaps, the eucharists in so many of our parish churches have to be stylized and conventional. But in our present enthusiasm for the small domestic eucharist we must not forget that a great Sunday eucharist still has an important role in the life of the Church, and even for inquirers. At a certain stage of their seeking they may rightly wish to be anonymous inquirers; and, according to Harvey Cox, the possibility of being anonymous is one of the advantages of living in the large secular city. Later on they may be glad of the small, informal, mixed group. For such a group can speak out of its own experience and help seekers to persevere through the disappointments and discouragements which are almost inevitable in that exploration of life which we have called prayer. This group of friends will be able personally to corroborate the words of Christ to the doubter in the *Pensées* of Pascal: "You would not be seeking me, unless you had already found me."[24]

[23] *An Order of Holy Communion*: alternative services, second series (London, 1967); the same liturgy is given in contemporary English in *Modern Liturgical Texts*, Church of England Liturgical Commission (London, 1968).

[24] B. Pascal, *Pensées*, vii, 554 (English translation in Everyman's Library edition [London, 1932], p. 151).

Jan Peters

The Many Forms
of the One Prayer

OUR ATTITUDE and reaction to the message of the gospel as the norm for our personal and communal existence shows at least three important facets.

Like any other conscious attitude or action, the human action by which we determine our attitude towards the message of the gospel has an intellectual aspect, an ethical one and one that derives from experience.

When the Christian says that God is his "father", this statement implies an intellectual assertion. The cultural and scientific environment in which he lives makes him mentally aware of what he means by such a statement. He cannot rest satisfied with a vague reference when he calls God his "father". His faith itself compels him in every age and every culture to clarify for himself what he really means when he makes such a statement. This kind of reflection on the intellectual aspect of man's attitude towards the faith is a matter for thematic theology.

Next to this intellectual aspect, however, there is also the moral aspect since the statement that man sees God as "Father" has moral implications. The conviction of God's fatherhood is bound to permeate the pattern of man's conduct. Whether we see God as Father or as the Absolute or as the Ground of our being, will affect the way we act. Here, too, faith itself demands a clarification suited to the age. This attempt at building a responsible and contemporary ethic on the act of faith belongs to moral theology.

Finally, the belief in God's fatherhood also implies an experience. This third aspect of the act and attitude of faith also requires reflection. For the act of faith does not stop with the formulation of one's belief or with reflecting upon such a formulation, but rather reaches its fulfilment in the actual reality of the faith, the experience of it.

This experience need not always be positive. Some Christians often express it rightly or wrongly with the negative phrase that "God is dead".[1] It is clear that they do not mean this expression as an intellectual or moral statement. The slogan is simply a way of putting into words the fact that, for them, the ordinary experience of every day is such that it appears as if God is dead. This also shows that this aspect of experience is not decisive for man's conduct or attitude, although it is certainly an aspect of it.

Right at the beginning I said that we could distinguish "at least" three aspects in human activity which we can reflect upon. There obviously are other aspects which make the human act the object of other studies, such as psychology, sociology or the study of human conduct. I limit myself, however, to the three I have detailed, that is, the questions put by faith itself to dogmatic theology, Christian morality and that peculiar discipline which is rather mistakenly referred to as spirituality.

In this article we shall have to concentrate mainly on this spiritual aspect, this spiritual experience, because when we speak about prayer we imply this aspect of our experience of the act of faith. This aspect is probably the most difficult to treat of theologically.

This difficulty is probably due to the negative slant of our religious experiences. We experience impotence, insecurity and threats, and find it difficult to reconcile this with a positive affirmation of God's sovereignty, of deliverance and redemption, of the protection we used to find in the Church. It may also be connected with the difficulty of discovering the unknown God along the paths that lead us to a god that was only too well known.

Our experience tells us that the god we knew too well is dead, while our experience of the unseen and unknown God is still too slight. It is only feebly felt as a religious and Christian

---

[1] As we have dealt with this in greater detail in our Documentation, "Secularized Prayer" (*Concilium*, Vol. 49 [British edn., Nov. 1969]), we refer here to that Documentation and its bibliography.

experience; more strongly as a secular awareness of the frustrating limitations to which we can only resign ourselves.

This genuinely experienced and recognized impotence of man can also be a religious experience. And this religious or Christian experience of man's inherent powerlessness in all kinds of situations is expressed in a human and Christian attitude which we call prayer. That is why it is hardly surprising that there is no point in cultural history or in the history of the Old or New Testament where we can say that prayer was invented. Prayer is taken for granted. Nowhere do we find an explicit justification of it. Prayer justifies itself in prayer, just as love needs no argument but proves itself in loving.

Prayer, then, is a specific level of Christian experience. In it the whole man acts in his conviction about Him who reveals himself in the New Testament as Father and as Love, and it is based on the conviction of faith that this redeeming God allows himself to be understood by man as the liberating and relieving response to man's lack of power. In other words, prayer is the typical act of man who realizes his impotence in faith. Or, in Jacquemont's striking phrase: to pray is to let the Word flow through us in such a way that it reaches the Father.[2]

In this sense prayer is the heart of faith and expresses the very breath of Christian life. In this general way it is still without form, but it can express itself as a petition, as meditation, as a prayer formula, and as worship. But these various forms of prayer are strongly influenced by cultural factors. I shall deal with this later, but want for the moment to stress the general nature of prayer with some reference to Scripture.

One might be inclined to attribute the way prayer is taken for granted in Scripture to a naïve self-understanding of man in the Old Testament or a myth-bound culture. It seems to me that there is a deeper explanation. In the Old Testament, prayer is an essential part of Israel's piety, which rests on the conviction that the bilateral relationship of the Covenant is real. That is why the exemplar of prayer in the Old Testament is Moses, since for him prayer is explicitly linked with the rise of Israel as God's own people (Ex. 33. 17; Num. 11. 12).

[2] P. Jacquemont, *Oser prier ou l'originalité du chrétien* (Paris, 1969).

Every important fact is preceded by prayer and followed by thanksgiving (2 Sam. 7. 25; 2 Chron. 14. 10; 2 Macc. 15. 14). The Psalms bring out in the form of prayer the same deeds of salvation and promises which are related in the historical books. They do not simply duplicate the historical books, any more than the prophets do.

These deeds of salvation are narrated as events in the historical books, related to the future in the prophetic books, and put in the optative mood in the Psalms. Modern linguistic analysis has made us aware of these three ways of using language as corresponding to authentic human aspects of man's attitude to reality. In the Old Testament, prayer has the features of intercession and stresses the aspects of promise and of relatedness to the future. The New Testament says no more about the necessity of prayer than the Old. It is rather seen as a privilege, something man can do in spite of his impotence. Man is not crushed by his impotence but can use it in a religious way which does not alienate him from himself, and yet lifts him above himself.

The New Testament shows prayer as the expression of man's relation to God. Of this the *Our Father* is the paradigm (Luke 11. 2 f. and Matt. 6. 9–13). Just as the Psalms express the message of salvation in the optative mood, so the *Our Father* puts the reality of salvation in the optative, in the form of a prayer, and has been strikingly described by the Fathers as a "summary of the whole gospel" (*breviarium totius Evangelii*), but in the optative. For Jesus himself, prayer is closely linked with his mission or with the formation of his disciples: at baptism (Luke 3. 21); at the choice of the Twelve (Luke 6. 12); at the transfiguration, the dialogue between the Old Testament (Moses, the law and Elijah, the prophet) and the New Testament (as the fulfilment of the law and the prophets in Jesus); before his passion (Mk. 14. 36), and elaborated in the praying, not narrative, form of the sacerdotal prayer by the contemplative evangelist, John (16 f.). The resurrection is understood as the Father hearing Jesus' life of prayer, and so Jesus becomes the intercessor for his brethren (Heb. 7. 27). But this intercessor remains present to his people (cf. Luke 24. 53; Acts 5. 12).

In the primitive Church, too, prayer precedes important happenings, follows these as thanksgiving and accompanies the daily life of the Church in the form of liturgical celebrations. Paul links this prayer, which plays an important part in his personal life as well as in his personal mission (cf. Rom. 15. 30 f.), with the sending of the Spirit, the Spirit of Jesus, who enables the believer to conduct himself as "child of God" (title used for Israel as the chosen people) and thus to belong to the true Israel according to the Spirit. The writings of the New Testament end with a prayer and so once again emphasize the "optative" character of the realities of the New Testament. The various traditional forms of prayer, such as intercession, adoration, communal prayer, liturgical prayer, petition and meditative prayer, appear already in a rudimentary way in the New Testament.

Christian prayer in the New Testament is pre-eminently altruistic and concentrates on God's will as effectively tending towards the salvation of his people, at every level. It sharply rejects the pagan prayer which tries to make the gods come round to one's own views (*fatigare deos*). In contrast, Christian prayer makes clear that prayer is not the same as exorcizing the power of the divinity but rather the expression in faith of that real impotence which besets man when he listens to the Sermon on the Mount and when he realizes that the kingdom of God will come as salvation, not as a matter of force and fate.

It is against this background of salvation as preached that the basic urgency of prayer becomes manifest. Prayer is indeed a basic element for Christianity. But it is only when this basis is notably lacking, namely, when what is founded on this basis threatens to collapse, that the necessity of such a basis becomes evident.

At this point we can observe a certain need for prayer in our age. And the best way of approaching this is by following von Hügel[3] who has pointed out the various complementary elements of religiousness. All great religions show at their best periods an intertwining of worship, doctrine and ethics. There are ritualistic

---

[3] F. von Hügel, *The Mystical Element of Religion*, 1 (London, 1908). Society wants religion to articulate any experience for which society itself has no language. The opposite seems also to be true: when the experience of prayer in the Church has atrophied, it seeks an outlet in sects, or, in a secularized form, in a new literary genre, the private diary; cf. A. Girard, *Le journal intime* (Paris, 1963), pp. xi–xvii and 601–5.

religions or forms of religiousness which in fact reduce religious life to a collective participation in certain external acts of worship. There is a dogmatic religiousness which sees religion too exclusively in the rational acceptance of an orthodox confession. There is the ethical approach that seeks to reduce religious life to a definite system of morality. And there is also a religiousness which only stresses prayer, mystical introversion or religious experience.

When any of these various emphases becomes exclusive, the sanity as well as the liberating and redeeming aspect of religion is threatened. Then we get ritualistic petrifaction, dogmatic formalism, moral secularization or narrow-minded secularization, mystical evaporation or spiritual alienation. And while we may speak about a theological revival in the field of thematic and moral theology, we are at a loss in the field of spirituality. Yet, this spirituality—and under this heading I range prayer in all its cultural manifestations—will only begin to grow again in the soil of doctrinal and moral thought if we do not want to drop to the level of magic prayer which tries to "force" reality, and recalls the Faustus-like elements that are present in all cultures, or to that of oppressiveness which is induced by external compulsion.

The true necessity of prayer lies in the Christian message itself. There is no other way in which the Christian, who experiences his fundamental impotence with regard to this message, can genuinely express his definite conviction about his origin and his future, and the inner possibility of self-realization and authentic deliverance. Without this, the dogmatic and moral elaboration of his faith would simply become either an ideology or a form of gnosticism.

Now, it is of course possible to be convinced of the need for prayer and yet realize that one is unable to pray. In theory it is clear that for a Christian prayer is possible. This possibility is implied in the fact that the Christian message is essentially a dialogue, an exchange: God wants to save us, and *does* save us, on the basis of a covenant between him and us. In the Christian faith there is always a mutual, personal relationship. In Christianity, salvation is never thought of as coming from some anonymous "elsewhere" but from an actual personalist reality. If our profession of faith recognizes Jesus as the one who fulfilled the promise contained in revelation, then a dialogue with this Jesus must be possible, there must be a presence with which we can have contact, and it must be possible to hear this Word anew as revelation of the Father.

We can also adduce anthropological arguments for the possibility of prayer. Man is the creature that constantly overcomes his limitations: he turns sounds into language; he turns noise into music, *eros* into *agape*, individuals into community, fallow land into cornfields, and distance into neighbourhood. He is never satisfied with the world as it is but always strives after the world he wants, and with a certain success. And so he also constantly transcends his fundamental impotence. The religious way of doing this is by praying.

He also experiences his impotence in the fact that so far he has failed to turn the historical reality of the Church into what the gospel means by the Kingdom of God, and that he has also failed to achieve that inner freedom which would allow him to claim that he lives in the freedom of the children of God. Now, are these limitations such that he has to resign himself to them or can he express and overcome them in prayer?

Not without reason, we opt naturally for this latter attitude and so come to the "official prayer of the Church" which can correct both the exclusively juridical view and the recent view of the liturgy as only a happening: if something happens, there is the gospel, the Church and the liturgy.

The distinctions between private and public prayer, liturgy and para-liturgy, devotion and official prayer, objective liturgical piety and subjective religious inventions, and so on, are not quite so obvious as we are told, particularly when we keep in mind what has been said so far.

The distinctions can no doubt be useful, and can be understood when one takes for granted that there is such an official institution as the Church which uses definite acts of worship and lets the other forms of prayer be what they appear to be in the eyes of the institution: subjective expressions of personal piety which must be judged for their orthodoxy and degree of permissiveness by this "objective" prayer of the "Church". But this comes suspiciously close to what in some sectors of society is called "the art of statesmanship".

The Church prays truly wherever the people of God pray as suggested above, where the Christian community is aware of its impotence to achieve the Kingdom of God in our present culture, where Christians see themselves as "only apprentices of the gospel". Whether this takes place in a particular framework, in a "sacred" building, according to an official formula or in the family, in groups, or through the spontaneous creativity of the faithful is secondary in so far as prayer is concerned.

The main thing is that prayer takes place and that it is inspired by a believing attitude towards the Good News. Wherever it takes place it will have to be borne by the Church's training for prayer. The many psychological differences, the changing situation, a man's own specific character and temperament of which the popularization of the human sciences has made him more conscious, all this will already lead to variety in the forms which prayer will take. Yet, all these forms are but variations on the basic theme of man, conscious of his inadequacy in the context of his faith. That this experience of his limitations differs from that of the Middle Ages, and lies now in the direction of a Church of the poor or in the obvious need for political commitment, is of secondary importance. What counts is that the Christian today sees these new limitations also in the light of the gospel.

One can naturally ask whether it is necessary to experience these human limitations, as individuals, or as a group, or simply as faced with new tasks, in the faith; whether it is not enough calmly to accept these limitations and to do one's best, or, as happened in the past, to resign oneself to them "in God's name".

There is no question of a real "must" in this question of prayer because prayer always takes place in the context of what we "may" do, or "can" do, of privilege and of possible creativity. To turn prayer into a commandment has probably been the most paralysing factor in the culture of prayer. It can only develop in the context of privilege, not in the framework of regulations. Hemmed in by compulsion, creativity languishes, and the ability to admire is killed by the habit of taking things for granted. But while our impotence is obvious enough, prayer cannot be taken for granted. We have probably been living for too long on the rich capital of prayer bequeathed to us by twenty centuries of Christianity, and we have not bothered to look ahead and to prepare ourselves for the time when "the word of God would become scarce" (cf. 2 Kings 14); not a crumb can be wasted. We have been spoilt by the wealth of our prayers and so discover no new ones. This needs qualification, because there is still always the question whether the experience-in-faith of our impotence, referred to above as the basis of our prayer, is possible at all in our age.

Vergote,[4] who made a survey of belief among intellectuals, had to conclude that they not only had no religious experiences but even mistrusted such experiences. They knew too much (or knew much too superficially?) about religion as "consolation", or as a projection, or as camouflaged self-centredness. Modern forms of prayer show more clearly than past ones that prayer does not lie primarily in asking "What use is God to me?", but rather in a growing consciousness of the question, "What use am I to God?", and here "I" must be understood collectively: "we, men".

Perhaps I should clarify the word "experience". When talking about "experience" I am not referring to feelings, or to some kind of identification between an awareness or an event on the one hand, and a theological statement on the other. What I am ultimately concerned with is whether in the process of our growing awareness we somehow experience, or better, share in, the redemption and deliverance as real, in other words, I am talking about an aspect of a Christian anthropology.

Theology must be certain that in its reasoning it responds to man's real existence, otherwise there will be intellectual alienation. If theology dealt with something that takes place outside the sphere of human experience, it would only alienate man from himself. Nor can theology simply take over what has been said better elsewhere (for instance, in psychology or economics, etc.) about man. It must bring man to a consciousness of a depth in his existence which otherwise is only present in a non-reflective act of faith or in a conscious act of unbelief, namely, the experience of impotence in the Christian sense. If it does not do so, it will shrivel up as theology, and, by the same token, the opportunity

[4] A. Vergote, "Christendom en ritus", in *Tijdschrift voor Liturgie*, 52, 1 (Jan. 1968), pp. 52 and 53; A. Dumas, "Dieu de la réalité et la réalité de Dieu", in *Esprit* (Nov. 1968), pp. 553-76; K. Rahner, "Glaube und Gebet", in *Geist und Leben*, 42, 3 (June 1969), pp. 179 and 183-4.

of building up a spirituality for our age will be lost. Experience by itself does not necessarily contain the principles by which to interpret its content in a Christian sense.

Elsewhere in this issue a new "prayer culture" is shown to emerge at every level of "God's people on the way". This does not mean that the crisis is over: one swallow does not make a summer. Yet, in a modest way these new attempts are a sign which cannot be misunderstood: a new way towards prayer is being discovered, however laboriously. The new rational understanding of man has not managed to make man totally intelligible to himself or to his fellow men. He can no longer afford the same naïve relationship with God since Freud as he indulged in before Freud. But this new knowledge does not make it impossible to achieve an authentic intimate relationship with God and a genuine experience-in-faith of his limitations. Even after the discoveries of psycho-analysis, man can genuinely experience his dependence on God—described by the words "child of God". As in the past, modern man still seeks closer union with a reality that is greater and more personal than himself, and the way to this union starts from that reality which man has always called love. This reality is experienced in faith as God: God is love.

The problem of the Church's public prayer is epitomized in the opening of the *Our Father*: how can we, freed from all illusions, speak with an authentic conscience of a reality addressed as "Father" and invoked communally as "*Our* Father" in prayer. This reality cannot be human fellowship as such, since the fellow man is not worthy of adoration and is not absolute. Nor can we bestow this name on the dark, and real, factors which largely determine man's growth as a human being. We can only say "Our Father" because we know that this does not alienate us from ourselves but rather brings us closer to ourselves.

Prayer is but one aspect of life. Based on our experience of the life of faith, as both human beings and Christians, it implies many other elements which belong to human culture and which have not been mentioned here, or only *en passant*. From petition to contemplation, prayer is a selective expression of our situation in life. This selection is not meant to stress one part of reality at the expense of another, but aims at penetrating the one and deepest dimension of all reality. It is a selection that cannot be limited to the superficial, transitory or immediately achievable. It is rather a positive appreciation of the relative quality inherent in the values of this earth, and it gives a deeper sense to these values by seeing them in their fundamental orientation towards salvation. In this sense we "read" the reality in prayer (*lectio spiritualis*), we penetrate its meaning as a sign (symbolism), and so we try to make the presence of the transcendent God, veiled in this prayer, visible to God's community and to all men.

Translated by Theo Westow

Joseph Gelineau

Are New Forms of Liturgical Singing and Music Developing?

ACCORDING to the wisdom of ancient China "music unifies, rites differentiate; through union comes mutual friendship, from difference arises mutual respect. When music predominates there is negligence; when rites predominate there is separation."[1] Symbolic communication, with which liturgical communication is connected, introduces the element of "distance" into human experience. The experience is not abolished but the symbolic relationship causes the immediate experience to be transcended. The real is apprehended at a stage beyond the sensible sign revealing it. Its presence is perceived through an absence. In this way the liturgical signs lead us to admit that we have no immediate, sensible experience of God, but, in faith, and through sacraments and symbols, a more profound and truer relationship. In this sense, by accentuating the distance between the signifier and what is signified, rite instils respect for the Other.

Thus we must pass through immediate experience to reach the symbolic relationship. The latter is always in danger of becoming formal and meaningless if it lacks an immediate experience to assume and transcend. Liturgy, therefore, can be formal ritualism and alienating hieraticism.

It is here that music can play a special part. Music occurs principally and primarily as a symbol. "Aesthetic experience" on its

[1] The book of Yoki, quoted by M. Courant in A. Lavignac, *Encyclopédie de la musique* (Paris, 1913), Part I, Vol. I, p. 207. The semantic range covered by the words "music" and "rite" is obviously somewhat different from our own.

own (and *a fortiori* the sole acoustico-sensory experience) cannot be a rite. But while it is put forward as a symbolical relationship, it has far greater difficulty in dispensing with living experience, articulated language or ritual gesture. Unrelated to experience, words can become as meaningless as an automatic sign of the cross. And what about singing?

It will be objected that we have experienced much devitalized liturgical singing, singing that appeared to lack symbolic relationships—tedious psalmody, plainchant "propers" performed entirely formally and so on; the music propagated nowadays by the mass media offers no protection against these deviations.

In many parts of the world there is a further fact to be noted: those who are willing to attend liturgical functions are increasingly unwilling to sing *if the music does not relate to living experience*.

On the other hand, singing as an expression of the community remains an almost universal sociological phenomenon, nowadays as in the past. The characteristic of music and singing is the power of establishing a community relationship both in very small groups (as small as two or three) and in large groups (tens or hundreds). Although the communicability co-efficient is necessarily modified in accordance with the size of the group, it is far less variable than with bodily gestures or the natural voice, especially in the case of choral singing which produces as it were in the group a synergetic strengthening of the sound image.

Singing together removes barriers. It can be called a "family" activity. And, when the group disperses, it is the melodies rather than the words that remain in the memory.

A liturgy with no singing or music will remain rather cold. Words and the rite are enough to renew the covenant of the Alliance. But singing adds to it a certain communicative warmth.

I. Vitality and Forms of Liturgical Singing

In a gathering of believers, singing and music constitute a characteristic quality of the life of the group. This was accepted by St Paul as a matter of course (Col. 3. 16). Pliny remarked on it in passing (two signs—meeting together and singing among the Christians of Bithynia). Nowadays, in joining a congregation,

whether in a large church or a small one, there is no more revealing sign than singing; it is a sign of life and friendship. I mean
of course the *act* of singing and not the repertoire or the style.

For the *act* of singing is a once and for all event. Of course, the
event can lead to results; then, too, from customs and practice
the forms can be elucidated. This is what is handed down by
tradition and is gathered in the liturgical books. These are useful
reference points for re-creating the act. Their interest is to be
judged in accordance with their chances of success.

Now on this point, as on others, the liturgical reform (not only
of the rites but of the congregations which celebrate them) has to
face certain important facts.

On the one hand, recent tradition has provided forms of singing (responsories, anthems, hymns, forms of psalmody, litanies,
and so on) which exist to bring into play certain "functions" of
the celebration. Now some of these forms are no longer func-
tional. Thus for many people the gradual, performed in plain-
song by a *schola* at a sung Mass after the epistle, was nothing
more than a passive period of waiting, or even of boredom for
those with no ear for the melismas. Yet this piece of chant was
traditionally termed a "responsory". Why was there no "response"? Musicologists then looked back into history and discovered that a deformation of the gradual had taken place. It must
therefore be reformed and its form as a responsorial psalm restored with the people's refrain answering the singer of the psalm.
But when the authentic form has been restored, does the psalm
fulfil its function in our congregations? Is it a vital form of singing in which the Word is listened to avidly and provokes an
eager "response"? If not, why not?

On the other hand, we are surrounded by a musical and choral
life, not all of whose forms are equally meaningful and effective,
but certain of which unquestionably "function" in their own
sphere—the popular song that people hum, the record that is put
on the player time and again.

A form only makes sense in a context. It comes alive only in a
given cultural milieu. Take, for example, the contemporary Western cultural milieu; it will be seen that many forms of expression, which were alive in the Mediterranean milieu where the
fundamental forms of Christian liturgical singing developed, are

now atrophied or have disappeared—acclamations, rhythmo-melodic recitation (cantillation), melismatic *jubilus*, and so on.

These forms can now be encountered in other cultures in other continents, thus enabling us to discover what kind of communication the liturgy derived from them. But in our congregations they often appear archaic or exotic.

On the other hand, our cultural milieu possesses other types of musical communication, in current use, which are hardly or never produced in the liturgy; such are certain methods of singing (voice production, methods of diction), speaking to a musical accompaniment, the creation of a rhythmic and harmonic background with instruments; lastly, there is the considerably widened range of contemporary musical language.

II. Types and Forms

Nevertheless, in setting out this list it will be noticed that it is less a question of "forms" in the classical musical sense of the term, than of "types" of expression and communication. Actually the determination of a form implies a system of differentiation that is accepted and meaningful within a given culture. It is in relation to the system of classical musical culture that the forms of the fugue, suite, sonata, overture, and so on, are classified and analysed. It is in relation to the systems represented by the liturgical "rites" of Christian worship (Syrian, Byzantine, Roman, etc.) that liturgical musicology has been able to classify and analyse responsory, troparion, anthem, litany, and the rest, in accordance with the terminology contained in the liturgical books.

Now the socio-cultural systems of the historic "rites" are in the full process of breaking up. They developed in a relatively stable and homogeneous milieu and have now lost their differential significance in a pluralist and open society—unless they preserve an archaic flavour, which is the lot henceforward of "folklores".

The reform of the Roman rite (the only one which so far has reacted to the change in its socio-cultural milieu) led inevitably to the loss of certain of its historical Roman characteristics (for example, through delatinization), and as a direct consequence raised the whole question of the ritual forms. The fact of translating a Roman collect means the destruction of its literary form. The translation of an introit anthem means the destruction of its original musical form. That is why the new liturgical books are necessarily reduced to outlining the fundamental "structures" suitable for the celebration of Christian worship (typical structure for the liturgy of the Word, the eucharistic liturgy, and so on), and then to bringing out the meaning of each "ritual function" (proclamation of the Word, sharing the bread, etc.). It is necessary of course for these books to provide set models of prayer as well as ceremonial rules, that is, the Latin texts and general rubrics. But their form is no longer significant of itself as a Latin collect of the Gelasian sacramentary or a rite of exorcism could have been in sixth-century Rome. The significance of the form will only appear in the actual celebration taking place in a particular congregation.

When we talk nowadays of liturgical forms it cannot be within the framework of a differentiated historical system which our times no longer provide for the liturgy.[2] It is a matter, rather, of operational models for which certain *types* of expression and communication of the celebrating group are or are not suitable.

III. The Need for "Operational Models"

The liturgy can be regarded either as a *happening* (an event) or as something "ready made" (a ceremony). A real celebration is always both, history and document. But it can appear more or less as "happening" or as "ready made".

As a result of the general state of rubrical rigidity our Roman liturgy had come down to us as something fixed in all details. The invisible event of the *hodie* of salvation was intended and implied. But outside the fact of the congregation gathering together and the preaching, when there was any, almost nothing offered a visible sign of the newness of the celebration. And so it was the formal nature of the rites, the literary value of the texts,

---

[2] This is true, at least in an urban civilization. The case could well be different where liturgy has to be adapted to or inserted in more homogeneous and still closed cultures. Can certain transpositions be envisaged in this case from one system to another?

the beauty of the music, the perfection of the ceremonial which held all the attention.

Subsequently, from the need to translate the texts and through the rubrical changes, the celebration lost its rigidity. In some countries and among some groups there then appeared the overpowering desire for a place to be found for some expression of the actuality of the liturgical event by a return to a certain spontaneity in the celebration—individual or collective improvisation of prayers, litanies, gestures and singing. In this case the resultant form (its literary or musical quality) is hardly considered at all, but rather the intensity of the action.

Neither of these extreme positions is tenable in good pastoral practice. Ceremonial hieraticism can ensure a certain religious feeling or please aesthetic tastes but leaves little room for the sudden intervention of the Word of God and scarcely commits one to reform of life or spiritual sacrifice. The *happening*, on the contrary, produces a certain warmth; it arouses, but it requires exceptional qualities of feeling and runs the risk of remaining at the level of an immediate religious experience.

From the point of view of the functioning of communication with which we are here concerned, neither formality nor informality as such is enough. Take the example of a collect. To abide strictly and always by the written text in the missal will often mean the celebrant's failure to supply an effective lead to a particular congregation in vital common prayer. But to improvise the prayer on each occasion would mean running many risks—poverty of content or expression, repetitions, obscurities and even incongruity. (A similar analysis could be made on the question of the intentions of the universal or bidding prayer.)

Actually the president of the congregation, besides possessing the appropriate charism, must also have the art of formulating prayer. Like all art, that implies appropriate training (in the scheme of a collect, for example: invocation of God, motive of the prayer, petition, conclusion requiring Amen; in addition: simple language, correct content, contact with the congregation, oral style, clear diction, and so on).

Between the poles of absolute improvisation and use of the "ready made", the celebration requires operational models which at the same time allow of an authentic, creative spontaneity and guarantee effective communication. To communicate, every group needs codes; the operational model will be in conformity with them. But it preserves a certain freedom of movement in its functioning, especially the possibility of using *feed-back* for the benefit of communication.

IV. In Music and Singing

If speech can be a forceful expression of an event, so can music. By making far more use of duration as the medium of differentiation it connotes history.

However ritualized liturgy became, it always possessed in music its creative side. Texts were continually being given new musical settings. Even the performance of an existing work is always a fresh creation. Lastly, improvisation (especially on the organ) has never completely disappeared.

But liturgical music came to be excessively formalized. This occurred in the first place through the devitalization of certain "types" of expression which had been formalized. For example, there is the chanting of lessons and collects, which in itself is a matter of rhythmo-melodic diction in which the narrator or soloist makes free use of a "tone" in accordance with the message to be communicated, together with a necessary element of improvisation. This had become, with a dead language, an exercise in singing in which notes were fitted to the syllables in accordance with precise rules, or again, at its best a melodic *laus canora*, as in the preface, instead of the public proclamation of the *mirabilia Dei*. Similar observations could be made regarding the short responses, acclamations, *jubilus*, and so on.

Secondly, the romantic idea of an artistic masterpiece, beautiful in itself and giving glory to God by its intrinsic quality, acted as a corrupting factor on the nature of liturgical signs by concentrating on the so-called artistic quality what should be predicated of the quality of full communication in faith. The musical *work* took the place of the *act* of praying by singing.

It is here that the working model can and must free us from the dilemma of artistic pleasure and preserve us from the dangers of the *happening* pure and simple. On its own, neither music nor religious fervour is sufficient. A symbolic relationship in faith is required. For example, the cantor who sings the psalm between the lessons in the liturgy of the Word must not be bound to a previously existing musical "composition" that he will then perform like a piece in a concert programme. He should not, on the other hand, have to resort to improvisation (often very short!). But if he has a model on which to base his singing of these psalm-poems according to their lyrical form (parallelism, poetic rhythm, the art of conjunction and disjunction), in accordance with the meaning that the liturgy gives to them at that particular moment (its function), and in real communication with the congregation (according to its linguistic, and musical code of expression), he then has some chance of successful and appropriate communication. The musical form becomes relative and remains subordinated to the ritual action as a whole.

Before aspiring to produce musical "works" which would become obligatory, like the Gregorian propers or Palestrina's Mass, we need to reconstruct working models to carry out the important acts of the celebration which require musical accompaniment. These are acclamations, dialogue, proclamation, acts of meditation, petition and praise, processions, times of silence, and so on. These models can only be discovered, learnt and taught, made known or perfected, by means of performances or mechanical reproductions. But these are to be taken as an example, a formula for reference to be applied or adapted, and not as a work of art.

This approach to singing and music brings liturgical practice into close touch with living popular arts—like jazz, which also follows models—and certain tendencies of contemporary music (*musique concrète*, etc.). It probably comes close to the vocal practice of liturgical chant before it was fixed in a repertoire. The practice has been preserved by some oriental cantors.

If models of this kind are successful, the resultant form can be observed. It will then be seen that some of these are very like the traditional forms and that it is not quite so necessary as it was thought to find "something new".

V. Controlled Experiment

If the case is as stated, it would be useless to make a list of all the contemporary forms of singing and music in order to find which could be transferred to liturgical use. This would be only to replace archaism by folklore or modernism.

There is no other way than to experiment in an actual celebration. Here various types of musical expression could be evaluated as liturgical expression and communication. After a period in which the organ has reigned supreme, we have discovered that guitar and light percussion instruments possess advantages it does not have. After the dominance of a style of singing called "sacred", because it was "solemn", the use of certain rhythmical forms has proved of advantage for common prayer. On the other hand, electronic music offers a vast range of possibilities for musical reproduction; it would be very strange if communication of the mystery could derive no advantage from them.

But this implies two things; in the first place real technical mastery of the means of communication employed; and then a really spiritual examination carried out by the group of the effects of such experiments in an authentic liturgical project. Now we still have only a few experts in these techniques (hitherto not used in church); and few congregations, since they have scarcely emerged from a state of passivity or individualism, are capable of this form of examination.

VI. "Sound" and "Noise"

Among the new elements that can be observed in an evolving liturgical musicology we must notice, without being able to examine them at length, two phenomena which modify fairly generally received ideas about the music of the Church, namely, the importance of "sound" and the existence of "noise".

By sound is meant the total impression made on the hearer of singing or music. Sometimes he appears unaffected: a certain piece of music seems to him archaic, exotic, academic, skilful or ecclesiastical. On other occasions he feels affected, positively or negatively: it is "modern" or "youthful", "lovely" or "pleasing", "beautiful" or else "ugly", "vulgar", "irritating", and so on. Now this perception is not entirely conditioned by the work. The same work can have a different and even a contrary "sound" for the same group. That is, its meaning depends on a semeiological totality in which the nature of the auditory group, the place, the time, the background, previous experience, the kind of performance, etc., act together to strengthen or screen communication.

This apparently commonplace observation seems crucial in liturgy in connection with communication by sound. The musical work has generally less weight than its "resultant sound" in the celebration. If this is so, it is more important to keep in mind the psycho-sociological elements which play a part in *sound* than to discourse upon the intrinsic form of a melody. The effect of a piece of singing can be entirely changed, for example, by substituting guitar accompaniment for that of the organ, and vice versa, because in the modifications of the *sound* a threshold of meaning has been passed.

The second observation is that singing and music during the celebration take place in a "situation of noise". By this is meant the fact that the liturgical action is not formally musical, unlike a concert or musical audition, but that singing and music are included in a complex action whose guiding purpose transcends them in every respect. There are then not only the material noises of a congregation which is not just listening to music as such, but also the interference at a deeper level from attention given to something "beyond" the music.

Musical experience in the liturgy cannot be likened (as only too often it has been) to what a music lover listens to in a concert or from a record, or when he himself is playing an instrument. It is actually far nearer what is signified in almost all cultures by music at a celebration, whether religious or secular, or it even approximates to the songs, dance tunes and background music favoured in public places and buildings. Here again works and forms are relative to the type of stimulation aimed at and the model followed to obtain it.

The originality of "situational music" in liturgy derives not so much from the means of communication employed as from the meaning aimed at and the nature of the relationship thus established. Of course, not all models are suitable for it. But to be effective in their own order they ought to be real means of communication for those who are taking part in the celebration. This is the field of an important section of the investigation at present being carried out on liturgical music.

Translated by Lancelot Sheppard

Denis Hurley

The Bishop at Prayer
in his Church

THE English language is fortunate in having the word "leadership". It is outstandingly useful in designating the role of the bishop. I remember trying to find a Latin word to express the same idea for a speech in Vatican II, but without success. Whatever barbarism I employed had to be illustrated by the use of the English term as well.

The bishop is the ecclesial leader in his diocese. The big problem for the bishop today is to evolve from being an almost impersonal depository of ecclesiastical jurisdiction to being a personal exponent of Christian leadership. Our theology always taught that there were three aspects in the role of the bishop: the teaching aspect, the liturgical aspect and the jurisdictional aspect; but in practice most of the emphasis was on the jurisdictional. This occasioned that justifiable complaint in the Council that auxiliary bishops, like curates, were among the most miserable of men—the only right they had was the right to ecclesiastical burial. As a result of the Council, much more balance today is given to the teaching and liturgical aspects of the episcopate, and the jurisdictional aspect itself is understood less in terms of legal definition, right and obligation than as responsibility for pastoral guidance.

The distinction between the three aspects remains useful as long as it does not become a separation but remains a convenient device for purposes of thought and discussion, and the organization, concentration and delegation of effort. The three aspects of the episcopal role pertain to one reality and can seldom be separated from one another in the exercise of that role.

This is most obvious in the liturgical leadership that the bishop must exercise in his diocese. When the bishop prays in his church, besides being the leader in public worship, he is most emphatically teacher and pastoral guide as well. When I speak of the bishop praying in his church, I use the word "church" not so much to designate the material building as the ecclesial community of the diocese. The prayer of the bishop in his church has enormous importance in shaping the prayer of all those who come under his leadership: priests, laity and religious. The prayer of the bishop has ecclesial dimensions in his diocese and repercussions in the diocese of his *confrères* in the episcopal college, that he can never overlook—the dimensions and repercussions of liturgical leadership.

To pray as a leader of the ecclesial community involves a number of deep convictions that one must endeavour to put into practice. The most important of these is sacramentality, by which I mean the sense of mystery which is the very heart of religion. We cannot see God face to face, so we must meet him in mystery. The mystery is the created situation in which God makes his presence felt, and the sense of mystery is the human capacity for recognizing and responding to his presence. The presence of God is hard to formulate as a concept. Humanly speaking, presence involves physical proximity, but there can be no physical proximity in the case of the incorporeal Godhead. We have to fall back on the idea of communication. God is present wherever he communicates himself, his wisdom, his love, his creative power. Moreover, our belief in Christ persuades us that the divine mystery has taken on the additional dimension of the Incarnation, and that, as a result, it involves the risen humanity of the crucified Christ communicating himself to us, a communication that is the outpouring of the Holy Spirit.

Sacramentality admits degrees of intensity, as the communication of God admits degrees of intensity. The whole universe is sacramental because it enshrines the presence of Christ. The Church is sacramental in a higher degree because there is a special communication of Christ in his Church. And within the Church the supreme degree of sacramentality is reached in the Eucharist.

The bishop who stands up to pray in his church must be aware of this, of this mystery of the presence of Christ in which he is so deeply involved. As he looks out over the altar he sees a community that is a sacrament of Christ's presence. He is one with that community in the body of Christ, in the people of God, in the possession of the Spirit. He himself is even more intensely a sacrament of Christ's presence for that community, for by sacramental ordination he has a special responsibility for witnessing to Christ the Good Shepherd, who gave his life for his flock. As he looks to his right and to his left he sees the community of his presbyterium, the *confrères* who by ordination share with him the labours of the Good Shepherd, and lighten his burden and strengthen him with their sympathy and advice.

This is the conviction that should inspire the bishop as he prays in his church, and there are two things he must do about that conviction. He must cultivate it in himself and communicate it to those around him—in the first place, to his priests, and then, with them and through them, to his people.

Cultivating the conviction in himself leads to the consideration that, though there may be a distinction between private prayer and liturgical prayer, there is no separation; for one of the essential ways of cultivating the conviction of Christ's presence is by prayerful meditation on the gospel, meditation that shapes the mind and heart of the bishop for the times when he prays in public with his people, and for all the other situations in which he must be the sacramental embodiment of the Good Shepherd.

Communicating his conviction to others means developing to the utmost in himself and in his priests whatever human capacities for communication are available and placing them unreservedly at the service of Christ. The basic capacity is that of speech, speech that must be as clear, melodious, honest and convincing as it can be. The second important form of communication is singing, especially community singing. As we know now, there can be no real liturgy without it. And both these forms of communication must reflect a transparent faith in Christ, present and active in the community, and a manifest concern that the community may be led to a deep awareness of itself and of Christ, a whole-hearted participation in the mysteries, and a truly human and Christian recognition of each member by the others.

The bishop who prays in his church is chiefly responsible for communicating all this to his priests and people. But being human and subject to human weakness he may often have to learn from others too, from priests and from people. He must be humble enough to learn, so that he may ever grow in transparence and effectiveness as a sacrament of Christ's presence.

Jan van Cauwelaert

The Bishop at Prayer
in his Church

I HAVE been asked to give a personal account of my experience of prayer as a diocesan bishop. I shall try to do so very simply. First, I should like to say that as one who has also found it a constant struggle to keep my ideal in sight, I have every sympathy with those who time and again have to make renewed efforts to remain faithful to the practice of prayer.

I do not think there is anything very original about my prayer. By and large, it is in tune with the renewal now going on in the Church. It grows out of the clearly felt need for a community in which I can join with others and with them be united to the mystery of Christ living in his Church. My experience as a bishop seems to have accentuated this particular aspect.

I had the good fortune to be brought up in a family in which common prayer held a place of honour. It was imbued with the warmth and happiness of the home. We took part in the celebration of the important parish festivals as a family, and these were always followed by lively family gatherings. I remember very clearly visits from my cousin who belonged to the priory at Chevetogne. He celebrated the Byzantine liturgy in Flemish and gave us communion under both kinds. These family celebrations made a deep impression on me. From boyhood they filled me with enthusiasm for a liturgy of a community nature that was fully understood. The services at school, although carried out very carefully, I found rather irksome. Perhaps it was because they were obligatory. On the other hand, the Masses which united us at scout camp, in the tent, near the altar, gathered round the priest who shared our life in every way, the evening prayers round the camp fire, and the confessions we made strolling with the chaplain—all these left on me an unforgettable impression from which I have always drawn inspiration.

At the Leo XIII seminary in Louvain, we were trained in a spirituality closely linked to the liturgy. Our services were filled with the community spirit. The great freedom prevailing at the seminary, the trust placed in us by our superiors, and the example they set us, encouraged us to be open with them and among ourselves. The ideas of a former student of this seminary, Abbé Poppe, of whose writings we were ardent readers, did much to encourage this spiritual fellowship. It was also at this time that I came across Abbot Marmion's books, notably *Christ the Life of the Soul* and *Christ in his Mysteries*. They helped me to see my prayer as participation in the life of Christ in his Church, actually realized in a community of prayer.

Subsequently I entered the missionary congregation of Scheut where I found a particularly happy community spirit, in accordance with the congregation's motto of *Cor unum et anima una*. But its spirituality was based not so much on the prayer of the Church as on the traditional devotional exercises. My daily meditation on the writings of Pius Parsch, and regular visits to the abbey of Mont-César to take part in the services, fostered the liturgical spirit in me. In addition, I owe much to the teaching of a leading theologian of our congregation, Father A. Janssens. His treatise on the sacraments was based far more on a thorough study of patristic tradition than on the scholastic theories.

Shortly after my arrival in the Congo I was put in charge of a school and also given the visiting of the neighbouring villages. My prayer at this time was inspired by my efforts to get my pupils, the Christians and the catechumens, to take part in the great prayer of the Church. In those days possibilities were very limited. But inspired by the need to remain in communication with others during the celebrations, ways were found of establishing a real praying community. Principally, I made use of commentaries, exhortations, adapted musical settings, and a course of instruction all centred round participation in the liturgy. Though my colleagues complained of the distractions caused by these interventions, I found them a valuable aid to the intensification of my prayer as they kept me in touch with the congregation. I felt isolated when I had to celebrate alone or with a passive and silent community.

When I visited the Christian communities in the villages I travelled under very primitive conditions. This enabled me to enjoy the people's great hospitality and to share their life far more closely than I could at the mission station. I discovered from experience how much close contact encouraged fellowship in prayer. My long conversations with the villagers in the evenings round the fire, or with the catechist and my assistants during my journeys by land or water, were a great help to me; they enabled me to see into their minds, which in turn helped me to adapt the liturgical celebrations to their needs. At the end of a long journey my companions would sometimes say to me, "Now we understand you much better, you talk like one of us."

Sharing like this in the life of the Congolese, and these very simple but intensified celebrations with them, helped me to understand the life of our Lord much better. Consequently, I learned to nourish my prayer not only by reading the Word in Scripture, liturgical prayers or spiritual authors, but also by sharing in the actual life of the community in which I had to proclaim and celebrate the Word.

The renewal provoked by the great encyclicals *Corpus Mysticum* and *Mediator Dei* left their mark on my prayer life during a few years' teaching at the regional seminary at Kabwe in the Congo and our scholasticate in Belgium. I was also entrusted with the training of catechists and this brought me in contact with the catechetical renewal and I came to see more clearly that catechesis must be an initiation into the mystery of Christ as it is experienced in a community of faith, worship and charity leading to a commitment, a commitment of faith in liturgical celebrations in which such a community is built up. My whole spirituality, centred in this way on these great themes of the liturgical and catechetical renewal, was lived out in the community in which I had to teach. I felt the need to live the life of my pupils and to avoid any special privilege as their teacher. What for others might have seemed a great sacrifice became for me the source of real development; I felt that I was fully integrated in the student community.

When I was made bishop of the diocese of Inongo in the Congo I found quite naturally the community of which I was to make my life of prayer a part. But for me this diocese was not primarily a juridically constituted entity, but rather the whole of the various concrete communities in which I was to live with my colleagues and the faithful. It never occurred to me to have a private chapel. I celebrated and prayed with the community where I lived or which I was visiting. Although I always felt a strong need for recollection, and to set apart for myself times and days of silence to unite myself more closely to God, this never caused me to cut myself off from the community or its prayer. And so I liked to make my retreat in the most remote mission stations where every day I presided over the prayer of the faithful.

The first directive for active participation in the Mass in my diocese was the result of one of these retreats in which I lived intensely what I was going to suggest for my missionaries and the faithful. The meetings for the catechists or the leaders of the apostolic movements were very special occasions. Organized on the model of the Jerusalem community, they were conceived as experiences which the participants were as far as possible to repeat in their own communities. The celebrations of Mass and the Word, prepared by instruction and meals taken in common (the meals were prepared by the wives of those present) formed the basis of these experiences. I myself lived with them as a member of the community and I must acknowledge that these periods were as much for me as for them privileged periods for my prayer and my pastoral commitment.

What appears to me to be of principal importance for a bishop's prayer is that he does not merely feel himself more responsible than others to pray for those entrusted to his charge, but that he prays always in living contact with them through taking part in their prayer in an actual community in his diocese.

But as a bishop I felt that I also presided over the prayer in my diocese and was responsible for it. I always took my inspiration from this verse in the Acts of the Apostles: "It is not right that we should give up preaching the word of God to serve tables . . . but we will devote ourselves to prayer and the ministry of the word" (6. 2).

Following this principle, and relying on my colleagues for the organization of charitable works and teaching, I was always able to find the time to follow the catechetical and liturgical renewal; I was able to send directions to my missionaries and draw up a large amount of material for the progressive renewal of the liturgical life of my diocese. Everything that I suggested to them I had myself previously tried out during my visits to the mission stations or the villages of the interior. I greatly benefited also from their suggestions and experiences. But principally I was aware that this renewal required a complete change of mental attitude, the change from an individualistic form of devotion to a community and ecclesial spirituality which finds its place in the great tide of the paschal mystery at work in our communities. All my personal prayer was directed to deepening my awareness of this great mystery so that I could feed my flock on it and lead them towards the *parousia* of our triumphant Lord already at work there where two or three are gathered together in his name.

When suggestions were asked in preparation for the Council I sent in the following *votum*; it seems to me to express very well my own experience and the ideal at which I have always aimed.

> We expect from the Council in particular courageous directions for a reform of the liturgy. All the ceremonies of worship must be an expression of the fellowship of the whole community of believers with Christ. To this end, celebrations should be simple, clear, and popular. In worship, nothing must bring about a separation between the priest who presides in Christ's name, and his people. Everything must be understood. In that case, it will not be difficult to give the teaching of the faith its full significance as the proclamation of salvation in Christ. The cutting off of the clergy from the people will be definitively brought to an end, and the people will find in the hierarchy ruling it, the mystery of Christ, the head of the mystical Body, through whom the "whole body, nourished and knit together through its joints and ligaments grows" to maturity (Col. 2. 19). Each celebration will recall to the faithful the meaning of their mission; it will give them the strength to proclaim salvation to the world in our union with Christ, and to sanctify their family and social life in the service of unity. And so it will be not merely the bread that is consecrated to become the body of Christ, but the whole community. And then Christianity will again live the ideal of the Jerusalem community.

Translated by Lancelot Sheppard

Gerard Broccolo

The Priest Praying in the Midst of the Family of Man

INTRODUCTION

THE state of liturgical prayer today reflects the time of change in which we live. Under the guidance of the *Consilium* in Rome, most of the liturgical structures and forms have been officially updated. Nevertheless, through a lack of liturgical preparation and education in many sectors, the former attitude to and presuppositions about liturgy have remained largely the same. Many priests are trying to fit the new liturgical directives into the old legalistic frameworks, and find great frustration in the confusion and "lack of clarity" which seem to result. Others, impatient with the slow, gradual pace of the official changes, have abandoned many of the "prescribed texts" and immersed themselves in many and varied home-spun creations. In each case, there seems to be greater concern about the externals of the liturgy, whether comfortably old or refreshingly novel, than about its internal faith and prayer dimensions. For one group, the question is whether something is legally permitted, whereas for the other the question seems to be whether it is immediately meaningful. The *real* question should be: "How does a priest pray—really pray—in the midst of the family of man?"

In a subconscious attempt to answer this real question, some priests have, to the best of their ability, conscientiously implemented every directive of the legislated liturgical changes. They have faithfully executed every detail of what one is supposed to do in the "new liturgy". Yet, after the novelty wears off, their people, for the most part, seem as apathetic and unresponsive as ever. The liturgical changes were supposed to make their parishes into vital, Christian communities, and all the extra time and effort seem to have had very slight impact on the daily lives of their parishioners. Many priests of good will and pastoral zeal have therefore concluded that the problem must be with the pre-scribed structures and texts. They have created more "natural" structures with contemporary secular readings or spontaneous prayers, especially when in the more private, informal atmosphere of a home or "underground" Mass. In place of the venerable prayers of the Roman Missal, readings have been introduced from Camus, Berrigan, Sartre, Gibran, Kierkegaard, Hammarsk-jöld, Simon and Garfunkel, and so on. Extensive use has also been made of the more "relevant" texts found inside those colour-ful jackets of new books of contemporary prayers, such as those by Michel Quoist, Malcolm Boyd, Huub Oosterhuis, Louis Evely or Douglas Rhymes. But disillusionment seems to be infecting even these liturgies of creative initiative, and men are walking away almost convinced that one of the most beautiful human needs, that of ritual celebration, is itself irrelevant and *passé* for modern man. Concern for liturgy has already been abandoned by some *avant-garde* groups, and wholly replaced by discussion and social action.

In the midst of such contemporary malaise, it is necessary to take a long, hard look at just what the liturgical prayer of the priest celebrant is supposed to be. What criteria can be set for determining the long-term success or value of the officially legis-lated attempts and privately initiated efforts to make liturgy come alive? Those who hold the priestly office and possess the "charism of community leadership" will feel the urgency of this crisis.[1] For many priests today, the question is no longer whether some-thing is legally right or wrong. Nor is it a question of whether a particular liturgical form stimulates a meaningful feeling of relevancy or excitement. *The real question is how a priest can be spiritually effective in his role as the leader of community prayer.*

[1] For a dogmatic explanation of the priestly "charism of community leadership" see W. Kasper, "A New Dogmatic Outlook on the Priestly Ministry", in *Concilium* 43 (1969), pp. 20–33; British edition, March 1969.

I. The Leader of Community Prayer

Priest as Spirit

In an attempt to respond to this question, I would suggest that the initial key might be found in an understanding of the priest as an *"alter Spiritus"*.[2] For years we have considered the priest as an *alter Christus*, as someone wholly configured to Christ. While this is true, it seems to be the common vocation of every Christian, every member of the priestly people of God. Perhaps it might be more fruitful to view the priest as a "sacramental personification" of the Holy Spirit.[3]

There is a great similarity between the function and mission of the Holy Spirit in building up the new creation of the family of man and the role of the priest in the midst of the human family. Just as the Spirit transmits God's gifts to man, so the priest fathers the Word by communicating the divine mysteries of salvation to the human family. He does this when he reveals the primacy of catholic charity in his availability to all men, their needs and concerns. Similarly, he personifies the Spirit when he consoles, encourages, gives guidance and support, convicts the world of sin, and teaches and shares the Christian vision of human existence. Even though other Christians can frequently minister to the human family in some of these same ways, the priest has been given the specific charism of office to do so.[4] In the Sacrament of Order, the Church invokes God to bestow a special, prophetic charism of the Spirit upon a man in whom the spirit of a leader of community is publicly recognized, similar to the case of Joshua in the Old Testament (Num. 27. 15-20); in this way *the priest receives a public deputation to personify the Spirit in the midst of the family of man.*

A summary of the pastoral activity of the priest closely resembles the work commonly predicated of the Holy Spirit.

---

[2] The constant reference in this present article to the priest's relationship to the Spirit in no way excludes, ignores or denies his relationship to Christ. For there is only one Spirit, the Holy Spirit of Jesus Christ.

[3] One might find it pastorally interesting, for instance, to substitute the word "priest" for "Spirit" in reading through John 14-17.

[4] Cf. C. Spicq, *Spiritualité 'Sacerdotale d'après Saint Paul* (Paris, 1954), pp. 51-71, where he comments on the "grace" and "public function" of the priesthood.

In St Paul, the Holy Spirit is the Spirit of the Son whom God has sent (Gal. 4. 6), and it is this Spirit who warms hearts with divine love (Rom. 5. 5), and who produces by his own profound activity all virtues (Gal. 5. 22). He sanctifies and regenerates the children of God in baptism (Tit. 3. 5), and infuses into them the filial sense by which they appeal to God as their Father (Gal. 4. 6; Rom. 8. 15). To belong to Christ, one must possess this Spirit (Rom. 8. 9). He is the Spirit of divine life (Rom. 8. 2); he gives life to the soul and resurrects the body (Rom. 8. 11). Every supernatural activity among the members of Christ is his work; he is even the hidden source of all power in prayer (Rom. 8. 26–7). He is the source of the interior life within men, and of all supernatural understanding of Christ (Eph. 3. 14–21). Through him we walk from glory to glory in our progressive configuration or assimilation to Christ (2 Cor. 3. 18). Through the impulse of the Holy Spirit the Church yearns for its ultimate and perfect union with Christ (Rom. 8. 23).[5]

This comparison of the mission of the Holy Spirit with the pastoral activity of a priest is not idealistically unreal for people whose parishes have been blessed with a priest who is a "man of God for others".[6] In his first assignment to a parish, the author of this present article was privileged to have such a pastor, a man who truly gave "soul" and "resurrection" to the sufferings and trials of many of his people, who warmed hearts with his authentic concern for others, and who brought many "virtues" to life in his parish by his own profound activity of consoling, teaching wisdom and being an advocate. When we encounter such a priest who is living the primacy of universal charity, we can acknowledge most readily this configuration of priest to Spirit.

Role of the Spirit in the Eucharist: Role of Priest

Perhaps this configuration to the Spirit can be best seen in the comparison of the eucharistic roles of the Spirit and priest. The role of the president of the Christian assembly not only resembles but actually "sacramentalizes" or *mediates* the role of the Holy Spirit in the eucharistic action (which latter role has for too long

---

[5] J. Powell, *The Mystery of the Church* (Milwaukee, 1967), pp. 39–40.
[6] Cf. the fine description of the nature and function of a priest in M. Bourke, "The Catholic Priest: Man of God for Others", in *Worship*, 43 (1969), pp. 68–81.

been neglected in the eucharistic theology of the West). The
Spirit is invoked to make the Body of Christ come alive in the
midst of the worshipping assembly and to fructify the unity, faith
and harmonious love of the communicants. It is precisely the
priest who embodies, who "incarnates" this action of the Spirit.
His person, words and actions are the vehicle of the Spirit's
activity.

Moreover, the priest executes this role in the liturgical setting
because this is actually his function in the total life of the Church.
The priest must fulfil the same role in the daily life of a human
community if his liturgical activity is to ring true. The priest is
the logical and natural person to preside in the liturgical gatherings of a community because of his Spirit role in building up the
family of man into the one Body of Christ in the extra-liturgical
situation.[7] In the Sacrament of Order the gift of the Spirit is con-
ferred upon the priest so that he can inspire the Christian community to "remember" the Lord. He is the natural spokesman
in the Church's memorial action of the Eucharist because he ful-
fils the role of "prophetic interpreter" or "salvific conscience" in
the midst of all the daily events in the life of the Christian community.[8]

Priest as Spirit in the Prayer of a Community

If we admit this configuration to the Spirit as the foundation
of the priest's self-identity and spirituality, then we have not
only delineated his function or service within the family of man
(a person who becomes the community leader by his total availability for the demands of universal charity, because of his deputation to "inspirate" the ever-growing Body of Christ), but we
have also specified the modality of his prayer. For if he is by
public deputation of office an *alter Spiritus*, then *when the priest*

[7] Cf. Vatican II, *Decree on the Ministry and Life of Priests* (n. 6).

[8] In John 14. 26, we learn that it is actually the Holy Spirit who "reminds" the Church to "do this in memory of" Christ. The function of the
priest, by reason of the Spirit given him in ordination, is to stimulate the
Christian community to "remember" the Lord and the existential meaning their lives have because of his death and resurrection. This "prophetic"
role of the priest in terms of the eucharistic "anamnesis" is well described
by V. Joannes, "Sacerdozio in un tempo nuovo", in *Rivista di Pastorale
Liturgica*, 33 (1969), pp. 113-33.

*prays among men he must do so in a way that stimulates them
to pray.* Whether he is using officially prescribed texts in an
ecclesial liturgy or praying creatively in an informal situation
(*"ex abundantia cordis"*, or with the assistance of contemporary
prayers), his *manner of prayer* must manifest and engender the
gift of the Spirit in the people around him. Just as St Paul testi-
fied to the power and work of the Spirit in his preaching (1 Cor.
2. 4), so the Spirit within the Christian community performs the
eucharistic memorial of the Lord (John 14. 26). The Spirit himself "makes us cry out, 'Abba, Father!'" (Rom. 8. 15). The movement of the Spirit makes the Christian people sons of God (Rom.
8. 14); and unless they become sanctified as children of the
Father in their liturgical worship, the glorification of God we
predicate of our liturgy is of doubtful validity indeed. All this
activity of the Spirit, however, needs a human enfleshment if it
is to be effective in a gathering of human persons. This responsibility of the priest-leader of prayer to manifest and engender the
gift of the Spirit in the community cannot remain merely an
intellectual conviction, but must be implemented and communicated externally in a humanly tangible manner of prayer.

Godfrey Diekmann has written:

> How many of you can recall retreats in which the retreat master
> reminded the priests before him that they have been ordained to
> take the place of Christ, and therefore in no way may their personal
> preferences or personality intrude upon the sacred action. It is
> Christ who acts "ex opere operato", and therefore the celebrant of
> the Mass should, as it were, be a "faceless priest", anonymous. How
> far we have come from those ancient days ... emphasis on the
> sanctification of man means precisely that it is up to the priest to
> make the Mass such an experience that it really does stir the faith,
> and does stir, above all, charity. This is our ministerial task and it
> is a huge task, for it does not take place automatically![9]

For the man who is truly possessed by the Spirit in the depth
of his faith and in the human execution of his fundamental role,
the Spirit can be effectively operative even when he has to use
the prescribed formulas of the Roman Missal. For the real

[9] G. Diekmann, "The Liturgy and Personal Piety", in *The Priest*, 25
(1969), pp. 31-3.

problem today is not so much the written texts, traditional or contemporary, but rather the priest's internal dynamism of the Spirit which frequently is not communicated to the assembly in liturgical prayer. When an artist rejects as unsuitable every brush, canvas and set of oil paints that are offered to him, one begins to wonder if the man has any professional artistic ability at all. The growing disillusionment with liturgical prayer on the part of both those who follow prescribed texts and those who have experimented with creative endeavours, testifies more to the priest's inner inadequacy than to the inadequacy of the prayers themselves. All the new prayers and spontaneous insights in the world will remain liturgically ineffective in evoking a lasting response from the Christian community if the "prophetic interpreter" and "salvific conscience" of that community has ceased to manifest and engender the charism of the Spirit received through the imposition of hands.

Increase of the Spirit through Personal Prayer

In order to nourish and "to fan into a flame" (2 Tim. 1. 6–7) the gift of the Spirit which constitutes the identity and function of the priest, he must continue to receive in personal prayer what he is to give to others in public prayer. The language of the liturgy can build the family of man into the communion of Church only when it is born and sparked in a communion with the Trinity. Only a community can give birth to a community. The "man of the Spirit" (Hos. 9. 7) cannot father a prophetic discovery for others, when he has ceased to "wonder" in the silent reflection of his inner loneliness, or when he has not yet begun to pray together with the handful of friends who mediate the Spirit to him. The personal prayer of the priest must be an imbibing of the Spirit by meditation on the Scriptures, by deep reflection on his own identity and meaning, in the light of readings from theology and the *magisterium* (e.g., the Vatican II documents), and especially by communal and spontaneous prayer with his co-workers in rectories, houses of study, and so on. Only when he has drunk deep of the Spirit in such personal prayer can he hope to manifest and engender the Spirit in his liturgical prayer.

When the prayer of the priest is a reaffirmation of his self-concept as a sacramental personification of the Spirit, he is better prepared to pray—really pray—in the midst of the family of man. A man who fosters the vision of his self-identity and frequently renews the commitment of his mission as an *alter Spiritus*, gradually becomes filled with a contagious dynamism. The gift of the Spirit, given to the priest in the Sacrament of Order and revitalized in personal prayer, is not for himself alone but for the benefit of the community he serves.

> Anybody with the gift of tongues speaks to God, but not to other people; because nobody understands him when he talks in the spirit about mysterious things. On the other hand, the man who prophesies does talk to other people, to their improvement, their encouragement and their consolation. The one with the gift of tongues talks for his own benefit, but the man who prophesies does so for the benefit of the community. . . . Any uninitiated person will never be able to say Amen to your thanksgiving, if you only bless God with the spirit, for he will have no idea what you are saying. However well you make your thanksgiving, the other gets no benefit from it . . . any uninitiated people or unbelievers, coming into a meeting of the whole church where everybody was speaking in tongues, would say you were all mad; but if you were all prophesying and an unbeliever or uninitiated person came in, he would find himself analysed and judged by everyone speaking; he would find his secret thoughts laid bare, and then fall on his face and worship God, declaring that God is among you indeed (1 Cor. 14. 2–4, 16–17, 23–5).

When a liturgical assembly truly encounter, in their priest, a "prophetic interpreter" of reality, they respond with the "Amen" of their hearts and lives. In this way the priest's communion in the Spirit of Christ, which grounds his prophetic stance in the community, blossoms in the community's communion with God and one another. A eucharistic disposition in the people of God, by which all creation is sanctified, is the fruit of an experience—an encounter with one who mediates the Spirit, by which they can "remember" the meaning of their human existence and cry, "Abba, Father!" This contagious transmission of the Spirit cannot be effected by mere fidelity to liturgical directives or by mere exposure to liturgical innovations. It can only be achieved by *the inter-human dynamics present when an "alter Spiritus" prays— really prays—in the midst of the family of man*. The mystery of salvation today only becomes a reality when there is one whose "word", sacramentality and presidential style pierce the conscience of a community in the manner of an eye-opening prophet. The prophetic insight, which is the root of this prophetic action of the priest, is a gift of the Spirit—a gift which must be "stirred up" in the marrow and bone of the "man of God for others".

II. How Priests Pray Today

Contemporary Crisis in the Prayer of Priests

With good reason, therefore, those responsible for the formation of priests are concerned today about the prayer life of these men. The grace of spiritual leadership can only take root where there is an opportunity to express this externally. It is the basic principle of the incarnational and sacramental economy in which we live, that internal spiritual realities are formed by the external expression or signification of these realities. "Transformation in Christ is accomplished through specific sacramental actions."[10] Consequently, men who themselves do not pray cannot hope to inspirate prayer in the family of man. But as someone wholly involved in the work of seminary formation and clergy education, I cannot help but wonder whether some of the extreme concern about the prayer life of priests and future priests is not to some extent unwarranted.

It is true, and must be admitted, that some priests and seminarians hardly ever pray. Also there are priests who are not really praying in any sense whatsoever even as they preside at the eucharistic action. The Church of our times is suffering the dire consequences of this unfortunate anomaly. Nevertheless, it seems that seminarians and priests who are using *new forms of prayer* are far more common today than priests who don't pray. The critical issue is whether or not these new forms are equally as valid and actually as much prayer as the more traditional forms.

New Types of Prayer

For clarification, I shall describe five examples of these new

[10] *Interim Guidelines for Seminary Renewal*, U.S. Bishops' Committee on Priestly Formation, Part 2, Chap. 2, art. 1, n. 9.

forms of prayer, chosen at random, together with their former counterparts.

Firstly, there is the situation of the death of a loved one. In days gone by, the mourners would gather around the coffin and the priest would lead them into the recitation of the rosary. Although this custom was usually appreciated and cherished by the immediate family of the deceased, many friends and more distant relatives would often find the repetition of the "Hail Mary" a tiring ordeal, which they would try to avoid if possible. And the priest was very often anxious to "get through" the rosary as quickly as possible and be on his way. The results were usually not as edifying or spiritually beneficial as today when a "biblical wake service" is substituted for the rosary. The readings from Scripture, song and perhaps brief homily seem to be much more effective than the rosary for bringing truly Christian consolation and hope to those assembled at the wake.

Secondly, most of us can recall the praiseworthy custom in many parishes of having a novena service each week in honour of Mary, St Ann, and so on. There was real value in an opportunity to nourish devotional life in a manner other than that of the more official liturgies of the Church. This practice fulfilled the human need to express and form the emotional and subordinate levels in the spirituality of an individual or small grouping of Christians, so that their sacramental and strictly liturgical life might prosper more vitally in the larger, ecclesial community. Various para-liturgies are now being introduced as legitimate substitutes for such devotions. Although their purpose and result are frequently the same, these newer types of "devotions" seem more attuned to the culture and mentality of our new generation. In a McLuhan era of non-verbal, mass media communications, mechanically produced sights and sounds are being introduced, and rightly so, into the devotional life of (especially) our younger Christians. Consequently, we occasionally notice para-liturgical services which are almost psychedelic in form and most timely in content, e.g., themes of loneliness, estrangement, the need for fraternal reconciliation, etc. But so long as a truly Christian vision or orientation is present, these new forms of prayer can have the same spiritual value for today's

Christian as the older devotions had for his counterpart in the past. One important difference is that some of these new para-liturgies are far more demanding of the creative abilities and charismatic sensitivities of the priests who preside at them.

A third change in prayer form can be seen with regard to the priest's recitation of the divine office. Everyone knows the image of the parish priest, at the end of an exhausting day of labour in the Lord's vineyard, conscientiously and rapidly mouthing the prayers of his breviary before the midnight hour. His almost heroic endeavour in the midst of unrestrainable drowsiness pre-sented a picture which was both beautiful and sad. Emphasis on the communal nature of the Mass has been far more successful in effecting recent changes than any conviction about the choral structure of the divine office. Consequently, one cannot sincerely bemoan the practice found more and more frequently today of some priests who read and pray over Scripture passages together, even though they often do not "cover all the matter" prescribed in the Roman Breviary. Even though juridical directives cannot be taken lightly in an incarnational or sacramental ("institu-tional") Church, the spiritual nourishment which comes from priests praying the Bible together seems to be a far higher good when a proper hierarchy of values is acknowledged.

Another example of new forms of prayer can be cited in the case of contemporary compositions of Mass orations. Often the same sentiments and attitudes found in the traditional orations of the Roman Missal are expressed in these newer compositions, although the language has been updated. For instance, the oration of the Mass for Pentecost Sunday, in the Roman Missal, reads:

> O God, on this day you have instructed the hearts of the faithful by the light of the Holy Spirit. Grant that through the same Holy Spirit we may be truly wise and always rejoice in his consolation. Through Jesus Christ ... for ever and ever. Amen.

Whereas a more contemporary composition for the same feast reads:

> This is the day, Lord, when you give the breath of life to this world, when you enkindle a fire of love in men. Today is the day that we are called together to be your Church. We thank you with the words, the seed that you have sown in us and we admire you in

the power of the Holy Spirit and joyfully proclaim you as our father.[11]

Even though there may be serious legal difficulties with the use of such a latter text in a eucharistic liturgy which claims to be the liturgy of the universal Church, one cannot deny its merits as a true "prayer" for the contemporary Christian community. Although not officially approved for liturgical use, it is nothing more than a new form of the traditional prayer for this occasion. It is certainly not an abandonment of real prayer for something less than prayer.

A final example of a new form of prayer may be found in the instance of more contemporary compositions for the Eucharistic Prayer of the Mass. The prayer for the fruitful effects of the Mass in Eucharistic Prayer I (the Roman Canon) reads:

> Almighty God, we pray that your angel may take this sacrifice to your altar in heaven. Then, as we receive from this altar the sacred body and blood of your Son, let us be filled with every grace and blessing.

A more contemporary version of this passage reads:

> We pray, Lord our God, send over us your holy spirit, the spirit who brings to life the power of Jesus Christ. We pray that this bread and this cup which we offer you in humility may really be the sign of our surrender to you. We pray that in the midst of this world, and before the eyes of all people with whom we are united we may live your gospel and be the sign of your peace; that we may support and serve each other in love that our hearts may be opened to the poor, the sick and the dying, to all who are in need. We pray that thus we may be the church of Jesus Christ, united with our bishop and with our pope. . . .[12]

Once again, any objection to such a prayer would have to be couched in terms of the present legitimacy of its use, not its prayer value. It is not a case of a real prayer as against a non-prayer, but often merely of an updating of an older form of prayer.

Viewing these examples as nothing more than new forms of prayer, as are so very many of the prayers used by priests and

[11] H. Oosterhuis, *Your Word is Near* (Westminster, Md., 1968), p. 103.
[12] *The Underground Mass Book*, ed. S. McNierney (Baltimore, 1968), p. 47.

future priests today, should help to calm the distress of many who feel that our priests are no longer praying. Our fidelity to older forms of prayer should not be allowed to blind us to the possible value of some of these newer forms. Self-righteous defenders of the "forms" must beware becoming insensitive to real "prayer". As a matter of fact, both *avant-garde* progressives and die-hard conservatives are often guilty of the same fault: being more concerned about the external prayer form that should or should not be used than about the internal prayer value which can often be found in both the old and the new forms of prayer. The discernment, however, of what is and what is not real prayer is no easy matter.

Criteria for Evaluating the Prayer of Priests

The discernment of real prayer is closely bound up with the gift of the "discernment of spirits". The complexities involved here make the establishment of sound criteria for evaluation a very delicate and dangerous task. Nevertheless, despite the risks, three guidelines are presented here by way of conclusion, to help consideration of the role of the priest as a sacramental personification of the Spirit.

(1) The Manner of Using Prayer Texts

First of all, one must pose the question: "Are priest and people in this situation really praying or merely reciting prayers?" For centuries the human condition has demanded the assistance of written texts for its various liturgies and para-liturgies. To provide a liturgical aid without providing a liturgical substitute is no easy task. In his *Apostolic Tradition*, St Hippolytus provided texts, but with the instruction that these formulas be merely "normative": not "pray this", but "pray *like* this". This same mentality is evident in many of the rubrics of the new rites elaborated by the Liturgy *Consilium* in Rome. To say that *"Sacerdos ... sponsum et sponsam humaniter salutet"* is a welcome return to the type of directives that belongs in the "liturgical books". I hope the same mentality will soon affect the selection of texts and formulas as well.[13] Even though this liberty demands much

---

[13] A fine example of a liturgical book which stimulates real prayer by

sound education on the part of the clergy, many priests have already shown that they are worthy of this trust by the way the "Prayer of the Faithful" has been executed in many parishes in the last couple of years.

Nevertheless, there is still the problem that we have too many priests (young as well as old) who do not know how to use the prayers of the Roman Missal. "Am I really praying or just reciting words?" is a question no priest can ever cease asking himself. Moreover, he must ask this question of others who will give him an honest answer. Most of the time, while at the altar, a priest is praying internally and subjectively and *thinks* he is conveying this to the community. But in the objective order there really is no communication of the Spirit. Self-deception has never been more easy for the priest than today. This problem is not the unique prerogative of those priests who have been faithful to the prescribed prayers of the Missal, but is equally in evidence among some men who make use of contemporary compositions in the liturgy. The use of video tapes in training seminarians how to preside at the altar is an invaluable means of letting a man see for himself his effectiveness or lack of effectiveness in communicating the Spirit. Until this problem is remedied in the external order of human communication, all the remarks made earlier in this article about the man of the Spirit praying in the midst of the family of man are only intellectual concepts.

(2) *Evidence of the Charism of Spiritual Leadership*

Closely related to the problem of knowing how to use written prayers properly is the very common problem of many priests who do not manifest the "grace of spiritual leadership". If a man lacks the natural, human qualities of a leader of a community, if he is unable to inspire others spiritually, he will have tremendous difficulty in incarnating the charism of prophetic leader or salvific conscience in the midst of his people at prayer. Greater concern will certainly have to be given in the future to the need of this natural endowment before men can be selected for the

---

providing broad guidelines rather than obligatory details can be found in *An Order of Worship* of the Consultation on Church Union (Cincinnati, 1968).

order of priesthood. Not every man is graced with the leadership qualities of Pope John XXIII, Martin Luther King or Robert Kennedy. Nevertheless, if the priest is to be leader of community prayer, he must be able, at least to some degree in his own unique way, to inspire spiritual and Christian values in the people around him. He must be a man of vision, who is able to share this vision so dynamically that he evokes a response. He must be able to manifest and engender the gift of the Spirit when he prays publicly, or otherwise there will be no "Abba, Father" (Rom. 8. 15) and no "Amen" (1 Cor. 14. 16) in the worshipping community, because there is no Spirit "reminding" the Christian assembly to "do this in memory of" Christ (John 14. 26).

When a man with the gift of spiritual leadership prays in the midst of his people, he stimulates them to pray by his *manner of prayer*. The forms or structures he uses are secondary in importance. The five examples of new prayer forms given above are more reflective of a contemporary culture and mentality in their formulation; nevertheless, there can be no greater real prayer with these new forms than with the more traditional forms unless there is a man of the Spirit to make the written words come to life in an assembly. Only when the Spirit rises out of the community through Christ to the Father is there true Christian prayer. The voice of the Spirit is not in printed texts but in the hearts of God's people. By his prophetic witness, the priest must draw out this Spirit. In order to have real prayer, the voice of this community here and now must be heard.

(3) *Spiritual Effectiveness*

Some priests today are criticized for departing from the prescribed texts. But in upholding the legitimate discipline of the Church, we must not forget that these men are often more effective in stimulating the faithful to prayer and communion with God than some obedient sons who condemn but do not inspire. Christ himself has proposed the ultimate norm for evaluation: "You will recognize them by the fruits they bear" (Matt. 7. 16). "Pharisees . . . imagine ritual dispenses them from truth, and Communion from sharing; they carry their gifts to the altar but remain aloof and indifferent to their brother; they profess to love God, whom they don't see, and thus reassure themselves about not loving their neighbour, whom they do see."[14] The priest's task is to be not a custodian of books but a father to his people, giving them the life of the Spirit so that they may fulfil their Christian mission to the world. "To pray is to let God into our life so that he'll help us let our neighbour in as well."[15] When a priest mediates this Spirit of God into a worshipping assembly, both by his presidential style in the liturgical action and by his pastoral charity in the daily life of his people, so that they become more concerned about others, he is fulfilling his function as a "leader" of community prayer. Some "disobedient young priests", despite their insensitivity to the ecclesial and institutional nature of the liturgy, really are praying more to the spiritual edification of their people, because they feel more at home with some of the more contemporary prayer forms and compositions. There are also priests, however, who can manage the same spiritual edification while using the prescribed texts, because they are men of broader vision and greater "freedom". In either case, we must remember that a *spiritual quality* in the priest at prayer makes the difference. The prayers, forms and texts are of only secondary importance. It is the spiritual quality of the priest at prayer, not legal exactitudes, which we should commend or try to foster. Any judgment about the merits or value of a manner of prayer must take into consideration the purpose or scope of prayer. The goal of prayer, as the purpose of all liturgy and of the Church, is to be, to become and to build up the People of God. To the extent that the priest praying in the midst of his community achieves this goal, he has truly prayed.

Conclusion

The public prayer of the priest must be both a support and a challenge to the community's spiritual life. His manner of prayer must convey the fact that he is *really praying*, and not merely carrying out directives and reciting prescribed words. A sense of conviction and authenticity must be externally and tangibly communicated to the worshipping assembly. Most of all, his total

---

[14] L. Evely, *Teach Us How to Pray* (New York, 1967), p. 69.
[15] *Ibid.*, p. 85.

presidential style must be stimulating, inspiring the faithful people to prayer by his *charism of spiritual leadership*.

When a priest prays—really prays—in the midst of the family of man, he truly becomes the salvific conscience and prophetic interpreter of the worshipping assembly. The liturgical structures (e.g., homily, Prayer of the Faithful, and so on) provide the forum in which the priest's manner of prayer can "give meaning" not only to the communal, liturgical action but to the whole daily existence of his people. Only a man who is a sacramental personification of the Spirit in both his inner dynamism and public function, can accomplish the task of transforming the Christian community into children of the Father and into the Body of Christ. The priest must manifest and engender this Spirit, for it is only *the Spirit* who effects true Christian worship and prayer in the family of man.

Adriana Zarri

Woman's Prayer and
Man's Liturgy

IT IS rather difficult to discover any feminine values in the liturgy, and the results of any search are somewhat disappointing. One reason for this deficiency is to be found in the tone of liturgical language which is inevitably slightly generic; another is an understandable modesty which prevents the expression of feelings of a too private and personal nature, and yet another is its universal purpose which requires a very extensive common denominator. It would therefore be useless to look for a liturgy for men or women, for young people, for intellectuals, and so on. Although one can foresee a certain degree of differentiation in the future, what we have today is a community liturgy in which there is "neither male nor female" (Gal. 3. 28).

But there is another, more specific reason which explains the scarcity of feminine values, and it is this reason that interests me most. The liturgy has been made by men. Not only that. In the West, at least, these men have been celibates, and frequently to some extent undersexed. Although his was an extreme case, Origen can be taken as the symbol of a subtle psychic castration caused by that Platonic mistrust of the flesh which is a feature of the asceticism of men who unconsciously need to find some philosophical justification for their existential renunciation.

On account of this psychological situation and because of the historical environment in which they lived, such men were not perhaps most suited to understand feminine values or cultivate an appreciation of women. Their appreciation, when it existed at all, had a limited range and was somewhat rhetorical. They relegated woman to the home ("Queen of the hearth"), but she was subject to the male, given "feminine" work as the result of an atavistic sociological attribution, and barred from more important duties. Domestic and limited virtues were allotted to her. "Just as the instructions for the training of men are many", wrote a sixteenth-century author, "it is certain that the moral training of women can be limited to a few precepts, because men act in the home and outside the home, in private and in public matters. The rules for such numerous and varied activities require long volumes. On the other hand, the sole care of woman is modesty. When this has been duly explained to her, woman is sufficiently instructed. Therefore the crime of those who attempt to corrupt this sole virtue in woman is all the more execrable, like those who would attempt to put out the little light that remains to one who is already blind in one eye."[1]

Although such texts are obviously extreme, they show how slight was the consideration and the limit of the virtue granted to woman. Home, church, modesty, patience, and that's all. Courage, for instance, was no business of hers, and we can see this in the Collect for the Common Mass of a Woman-Martyr. *"Deus qui ... etiam in sexu fragili victoriam martyrii contulisti ..."*— where this *"etiam"* is certainly not a compliment, and the prevalent theme of divine power is contrasted with the concept of the special weakness of women, a weakness which is very common in the philosophy, psychology and asceticism of a masculine civilization which has lasted until the beginning of our time. This same concept is perceptible in the Mass for a Bride and Bridegroom, in which the bride is the object of special attention. But this is no compliment; it is the attention given to the one who most needs it. Reference to woman's weakness is not missing here either *("... muniat infirmitatem suam robore disciplinae"),* and the privileges which are granted to her are, as usual, of a domestic nature.

I. THE LITURGY OF VIRGINITY

The range of womanly virtues appears restricted, but women seem to have been given as a compensation the prerogative of

[1] Juan Vives, *Formación de la mujer cristiana* (Madrid, 1959).

virginity. Although a certain sociological climate explains this limitation, the sex and the situation of the liturgical authors will also help us to interpret this insistence. They were men and celibates, very understandably attracted by feminine virginity which seemed to be the best way of sheltering woman from unconscious desires and allowing her to be the object of idealistic admiration. Although woman attracts by her femininity, she is, as it were, made sexless, so as to purify the attractiveness and allow it to be worshipped. The liturgy seems to see in the Mother of Christ herself an abstract model of femininity rather than a flesh and blood woman; the same is true of that Marian projection, the cult of virgins. It is significant that whereas femininity is thus emphasized, a Common of male virginity is entirely missing from the Roman liturgy. Man's virtue is completely absorbed by other titles, such as bishop, abbot, doctor and (for want of any other) confessor, a qualification which women do not appear to possess.

Why is it that feminine sanctity gravitates towards virginity when it has no other titles, whereas masculine sanctity concentrates instead on witness? The answer has perhaps already been given. In a liturgy made by women we might perhaps have a Common of Male Virgins. At present we do not. When there is no martyrdom, no bishopric or theological doctrine, although virginity is available, preference is given to the confession of the faith (which in spite of being generical is admittedly a highly positive qualification). For women, however (with the sole exception of martyrdom), virginity prevails over all other forms of witness, and in its absence there is no "confessor", no "doctor" and obviously no bishop. One falls back (or at least one had to until a short time ago) on a dismally negative qualification—we might almost say a disqualification, because it did not qualify or only qualified in a negative sense—the office *pro nec virgine nec martyre*.

The situation today is slightly improved, and the Common of Lay Women is now available to those saintly women who cannot claim virginity or martyrdom. (It is perhaps not without significance that this negative classification should have disappeared at a time when a spirituality of marriage is emerging and the compulsory celibacy of the clergy is being called into question.) Besides, the women saints qualified with *"nec nec"* were rare cases.

There was not much hope of canonization for a married woman who had not been fortunate enough to suffer martyrdom. Perhaps she seemed a model difficult to imitate and above all rarely to be imitated; an unwelcome or even disturbing model. And, in the very office of these "holy" married women, we have the proof which seems to indicate the sexless and sex-destroying nature of the liturgical writers. It is certainly one of the least felicitous, and the Mass is the drabbest and most perfunctory of the whole Roman Missal. It does not breathe love, but washing-up and shopping-lists. Beneath it all, one senses a tension which has felt the need to gibe at beauty in a pedantic and sermonizing tone ("*fallax gratia et vana est pulchritudo*"), and to reduce the image of the loving one to that of a good practical woman, careful, thrifty and slightly mean, who looks carefully after her husband's clothes and enables him to cut a fine figure in the village.

Yet a male virgin is quite capable of meeting love with love. If he is relaxed and mature (I venture to say if he is virgin and not merely celibate; a negative virtue if it does not reach the level of charisma), he is in the best state to do so. Renunciation and distance, together with that healthy nostalgia which can quite easily co-exist with an unregretted oblation, would enable him to reach sublimation much more easily than a married man. Both in composing the texts and choosing the biblical passages (Why not, for instance the Canticle, which is now reserved exclusively to virgins, to the extent of almost taking it away from human marriage?), he might give us a splendid liturgy of married love, a liturgy which we lack entirely, almost as if we were afraid of it. Perhaps the liturgical authors were more celibate than virgin, concentrating more on the "no" to human love than on the "yes" to that divine love that, when it is full and consummate, no longer knows fear because it no longer experiences any antithesis.

In this insistence on virginity and on the neutralization of marriage, there is some indication of a very natural power of attraction which the authors vainly try to repress by elevating woman to a symbol as sexless as possible—just the virgin or mother (both unconsciously understood as a refuge from more intense and disturbing values), the sign of a love-hate relationship in which a celibate man often struggles.

II. Marian Liturgy

The cult of the virgin, which is based on a certain kind of anthropology, and exaggerated in a given psychological situation, reaches its climax in Mary, the virgin by definition; in the Mary-figure it is associated with the cult of the mother, which in turn can be made sexless—woman henceforth freed from love and almost excused from loving, on account of a procreative purpose. The Marian liturgy is not flat like the texts we have quoted, but it has a snowy, abstract and slightly frigid splendour; it is the splendour of marble, not the splendour of the flesh; the splendour of God, not the splendour of man and woman. At best, it is the distant splendour of a femininity which is not incarnate, in which Mary appears to us in an almost entirely theological light—the virgin, the "co-redemptrix", the guardian of heaven. Maternity itself appears to be considered only in soteriological terms. It is a basis for a disputation on the "theotokos" or "cristotokos", rather than a consideration of a real woman of this world. The Litany of Loreto (to quote a para-liturgical text) gives us an example of this removal of Mary from an incarnate femininity and her assumption into the sphere of symbolism. The most usual title is the bombastic one of "Queen" (no less than 12 invocations) which, surprisingly, is insisted on far more than the title of "mother" (6 invocations). Then follow a number of somewhat inflated and rhetorical epithets: *"rosa mystica"*, *"turris davidica"*, *"turris eburnea"*, *"domus aurea"*, *"foederis arca"*. Frankly, it is difficult to think of a woman as the tower of David or the ark of the covenant, just as it is difficult to invoke her as the "glory of Jerusalem", the "joy of Israel", "the honour of our people"; it is difficult even if we take into account the different taste and language of the Jews.

The titles of virgin and mother given to this creature of cosmic dimensions (*"mulier amicta sole ..."*) are frozen stiff by adjectives that keep her at a distance, like "inviolate, spotless, venerable, powerful", and a comforting "refuge of sinners" and "consoler of the afflicted" do not seem enough to restore more domestic dimensions to this marble monument apparently carved by a man afraid of women. But our search is not concerned with what is said of woman in official prayer, or with the way that prayer considers her. If this were so, I would have called this article "Woman in the Liturgy", and the discussion might have ended in a sterile and useless moan about the small place and scant consideration given to her. The subject is more precise: the prayer of woman and man-made liturgy; this involves a deeper discussion, which probes feminine prayer and—further still—the true values of femininity. It involves (if one does not wish to limit it to simple psychological empiricism) a meta-physical anthropology and sexology. Accordingly, I devote a part of my article to the ontology of the sexes, without which any reference to femininity might remain vague and gratuitous.

III. Ontology of Femininity

A discussion of woman obviously implies a discussion of man; she is compared with man and defines herself by him to the same extent that a man defines himself by her. The couple and man must be discussed in the accepted meaning of the human creature, a creature who exists only in a sexed incarnation—an existential specific in relation to a generic abstract which defines man essentially. The feminine being (like the male being) is not something accessory; it is one of the only two possible ways of being man, a fact which goes too deep for it to be reduced to a mere biological connotation, but which by itself fashions in parallel body and soul, biology and faith, works and prayer, so that, on account of the coherence which binds the whole person together, we can start from either pole to discover a homogeneous line of development.

We can also start from the biosomatic fact (as the one most evident and least subject to dispute) in order to return to the personal and personalizing dynamism which invests the whole man. If we want to start from this datum (the most modest one) the different sexual dynamics strikes us at once: in the first place, activity in man and receptivity in woman. One speaks of receptivity and not passivity. Precisely on this account we can talk of it in a dynamic sense, because receptivity has undergone an active reversal, while activity in turn has an immediately receptive hearing—a double and interpenetrating reciprocity. But when these concepts of womanly passivity are overcome, a certain initiation of the process is the concern of man. Woman begins her sexual adventure by receiving, a reception which becomes immediately active, but which has the roots of its own activity in acceptance. Morphology itself, which is so much more external and forward in man, intimate and welcoming in woman, with the dynamism connected with it, underlines these different positions, so that we can say that the system of giving and receiving virtually constitutes the physical and biological geometry of sexuality, to which a more spiritual geometry cannot respond by achieving the same positions on a psychological and metaphysical level.

Indeed, precisely because he begins by giving, man is initially subject. His position could appear privileged, were he, as subject, not determined in relation to the object without which he could not exist, as subject. He would be a meaningless, unrelated and nameless figure, waiting to define himself and to become someone through a relationship with another; to make himself a person through dialogue, which personalizes before it becomes interpersonal, and interpersonal precisely because it personalizes.

It is the object which determines the subject, making itself in turn the subject of that determination. In fact, we make *someone* rather than *something*. Together we make the object and the subject as persons. And we are persons, inasmuch as we make someone and are made by that someone. In this way, man makes woman and is also made by her. Eve (and we can use this largely symbolic name to indicate femininity) is born as a development and second stage of man; as the complete opposite of Adam; as his image, reflection and word; as a complete other self which, whilst being determined, determines him in a more existential psychology. Woman is the second half of man, just as the Son is the second person of God—a mere metaphysical indication without any hierarchical significance. Man does not give woman something of himself. He gives himself fully to her; he objectifies himself in her. Woman is in so far as she is expressed; if the fact of *receiving* seems to place her in a dependent position, the fact of *receiving everything* re-establishes her in a position of equality. Woman, like the Word, is second, but this *secondary* nature is, so to speak, *primary*, because it has no substitute in the parable of man, just as the Word has no substitute in describing the arc of the Trinity which infuses plurality into the divine unity.[2]

IV. UNITY, DIVERSITY, TRINITY

In terms of giving and receiving, subject and object, we reach the deepest roots of the being and of the person, which roots not only regulate a relationship but create it, by creating space through diversity. Here perhaps we touch on another fundamental feature of the couple. Woman, precisely because she is different, introduces a manifold dimension into a world which until then was monist and monolithic. Just as the subject as such could not be determined without the object, so man without woman could not be determined as male; he was merely the human creature—a generical and shapeless dough, not yet distinguished by sexuality.

Woman and sex arise from a virile type of amorphism. The historical and biological confirmation of a process which is so essentially metaphysical is of no great interest, although some confirmation must be given. Just as the multiplicity of forms developed originally from chaos, so perhaps the duality of the sexes arises from a sort of human chaos which we may call pre-Adamic, culminating in Adam himself, whom some Greek and Cappadocian Fathers, guided by Plato, saw as a primeval androgyne who with Eve gave life to sexuality. This may be a stimulating interpretation in a metaphysical sense, although it is somewhat fanciful and hardly credible on the historical and biological plane. But history was not the main concern of the Fathers and the biblical writers. In the words of Mircea Eliade, "Archaic ontology is expressed in biological terms", and it is possible that the first chapters of Genesis make use of biology as well for ontological purposes. We can read the first chapters of Genesis without examining the historic nature of the protagonists, who in any case are largely symbols and values, and as such may still be accepted

[2] Parallels between the human sexes and the Person of God—although expressed differently—are not new in theology. We have only to think of the parallels between Adam and the Father, and that between Eve and the Holy Ghost which, from Methodius to Gregory of Nyssa, from Gregory of Nazianzen to Ephraem, were frequent in the fourth century.

without being taken literally; and interpret them symbolically, as did the Fathers.

Adam, that cosmic figure, is asleep. In this sleep (which the old exegetes saw as a mystical state, but which can also be seen as the torpor of the primordial consciousness which precedes the speech of logical awareness), we can find an allusion to the pre-history of man: the slow biological preparation, the animal torpor which rises towards the awakening of consciousness, towards subjectivity and personalization, the gradual unfolding of the divine plan and the history of salvation, marching forward towards humanity and divinity, towards the first and the second Adam who sums up history. From this sleep, so full of meaning, are born Eve, sexuality, multiplicity, the story of the couple and of the race which leads the adventure of the world towards the ἔσχατον.

Woman is the intermediary stage of the human parable, but her mediation is permanent because the values of number and history which it involves (and which are the essence of femininity) are the everlasting flux that brings unity. Because—and this is the fundamental crux—unity is built with numbers, Eve, precisely because she introduces multiplicity, creates unity. Unity exists only as the synthesis and summit of multiplicity. Before multiplicity, there was no unity but only confusion. Here again the divine archetype helps us. If God is one, unity shines there in its purest perfection. This perfect unity is trinitarian. Multiplicity therefore does not break this unity but reveals its nature and, in a certain sense, its structure. The Trinity is the light of unity, its inherent motion, and its life.

We are now faced with a precise unitary reality that is not monolithic but many-sided, not monist but distinct, moved, not stationary but perpetually moving, a continual realization of the subject in the object, and perpetual rediscovery, unified at the summit in a "third moment" of the indefinite circle of the multiple. The multiple, which could be the antithesis of the one, were it not assumed in it, is instead its way of being. It is that which makes it free from any generic nature in an integral motion and discourse which give it life and reality. It is trinity which creates real unity, just as the object gives density to the subject. The becoming is after the being, but the fullness of the being is only after the becoming which restores the one to itself. (We might say that the Trinity restores God to God, making him consistent in a concrete, interpersonal and communal relationship.)

V. Woman, an Existential Dimension

If we apply these considerations to created reality, and especially to sex, we can attempt a metaphysics of femininity, which sees in woman the principle of multiplicity—with the adjustments (and frequently the tragedies) which it implies—and the premiss of unification. For she has a profound sense of history, and at the same time is disillusioned by it. She is sensitive to the horizontal, existential, incarnate; the call to receptive availability which exists in all creatures is particularly marked in her and a significant mark of her religiousness and the nature of her prayer. We can catch a glimpse of two different spiritualities: a virile, ascetic exaltation of giving, the strength of which lies in boldness and generosity, *and* a womanly ascetic exaltation of receiving, which centres on humility, candour, availability and listening; which—rather than take an initiative—is most attentive to the initiative of God. It is an ascetic exaltation tending to mysticism which sees in woman the privileged place of prayer in general, and of passive prayer in particular. Only now, after this initial discussion, can we compare liturgical prayer made by men with the specific tonality of feminine prayer.

In these prayers, especially in the collects, there is a kind of abstract stylistic technique (paratactic shape, parallelism, antithesis) used in a schematic, paradigmatic, wooden fashion, without flexibility and without existential warmth. The formulas are too global, generical and vast; they may be cosmic, but they are rigid, without the varied and changing movement of plurality. One prays more for man than for men. One senses the vast dimensions of humanity but not the living accent of singleness, with the individual name of each person. Created things are spoken of, but always in oceanic terms. One is conscious of heaven and earth, of the sea and of the cedars of Lebanon, but not of the threshold of home and the pot of basil (far better the passages from Scripture where, besides the cedar, we find balm and cinnamon and animals, each with its own life and its own lair, for instance the magnificent Psalm 103 which is read on Saturdays at Sext.

And there is hardly any prayer for the earth, and for man in his earthly dimension. Man is often only a soul—a concept which as we know is far more Greek than Christian and which nevertheless has considerably affected liturgical style. Even when it speaks (and it almost always speaks) of the whole of man, one almost always feels the vertical dimension. His relations with the earth are few and frequently exorcized.

The many collects of fear and contempt which contain an *a priori* refusal of time, the world and human experience, and which a woman would find difficult to express in the same terms, would deserve a chapter to themselves.

VI. THE PRAYERS OF CONTEMPT

Woman cannot reject time, for then she would reject herself. She may wish to escape from it, and she often does so, because the sense of history is not always accompanied by trust in history itself. Very often the reverse occurs, and those most immersed in time are somewhat disillusioned by it. But this weariness, wear and tear, and disenchanted gloom form a *consequential rejection*, the result of an experience which a woman goes through on a metaphysical and psychological level, if not on an existential one. Whereas man can give himself an *a priori* refusal which is not yet disenchantment (but a defence against an attraction, a not wanting to enter into a fascinating experience, and a fear of a life that has still to be lived), there is in woman a wish to escape from a disappointing experience, weariness of a life that has been virtually all lived, and disenchantment which withdraws from a too wearying path.

The *a priori* is the rejection of the beginning; the disenchantment is the rejection of the end. There is an entire existential experience dividing them, but only a literary nuance to distinguish them. This nuance seems to be absent from liturgical prayer, which is usually olympian even when pessimistic. It is an expiated and undramatic pessimism, where a feminine prayer would have been more sorrowful, dramatic and tormented, and would express not so much fear and defence, but disappointment with what has already been attempted. A man asks that he should be made to "despise earthly things and live heavenly ones", whereas a woman would prefer to ask "after so much weariness and disenchantment in the reality of the earth which we have uselessly loved, give us in the end rest with Thee who doth not deceive". Obviously prayers of this kind are also to be found in our liturgy (see for instance the beautiful and heartfelt *Salve Regina*) but they are not in the majority. Most, under the appearance of severity, often conceal a psychological attitude which is retrograde and infantile or simply utopian; they take up a defensive position or a leap towards God without human mediation; and express an ascetic mortification of existential curiosity, even when genuine, by a rejection of feminine dimensions, and not infrequently by a rejection of woman—a rejection much more logical than one might think, because God is the immediate future of woman, whereas woman (history, existential experience) is the immediate future of man. Therefore, the appeal to God can express itself by the temptation of by-passing woman who is, as it were, the historical and existential extension of man. This temptation is particularly noticeable in the celibate, trained to see contact with the feminine as temptation, and to interpret celibacy (erroneously) as doing without woman. A certain type of prayer seems to express, not just a male mentality, but one that is frequently immature.

Therefore man considers God preferably as an impulse and motive force, and woman rather as a drawing and finally consuming force (in the end as a resolutive refuge, and man instead as a protective refuge). Thus the many prayers that begin with the concept of God from whom we come, of God who gives (God, who hast bestowed, . . . God, who didst appoint . . . God, who didst endow . . .); whereas woman would prefer to underline the concept of God who cares for, God towards whom we are bound. It is evident that these two concepts overlap and cannot be isolated from one another. Nevertheless, even in their fusion, there is a different origin, prevalence, dynamism and tonality.

VII. The Prayer of Reception

But the difference in tone is even more evident in the case of the reception of love, and it should be noted that I do not say "of love" but "of the reception of love", which is a very definite way of loving. It is necessary to clear up a misunderstanding by which, through over-simplification, love is attributed to woman and intellect—largely—to man. But there is a different kind of intelligence, more active in man and more passive in woman. The misunderstanding also persists on the level of theological hypothesis when it is assumed that woman is more capable of grasping the reality of the Holy Spirit. I believe this not so much because the Holy Spirit is love, but because he is the Beloved, the end of divine love. Woman too wants to be loved, and one could make a large collection of prayers which reflect this attitude, and which occasionally find an echo in the liturgical sphere. Preferably, the liturgy asks: "Lord, make us at all times hear and love thy holy name" (Collect for the Second Sunday after Pentecost; one of the many in which this petition recurs). Woman, whilst having no difficulty in associating herself with such a request, would be more inclined to formulate it differently, expressing not so much her will to love, but rather her desire to await love: "Lord, make us to be loved by thee", or, more trustingly and daringly, "Love us, Lord"—a useless request from a petitioner's point of view, like all the most noble prayers, as woman knows well.

From many possibilities, I select the example of Sister Elizabeth of the Trinity. The images she chooses are particularly significant: "... I deliver myself to him like a prey",[3] like "a small cup beneath the spring".[4] The verbs she uses (continually in the passive) are: "submerge", "invade"[5] ("let us be invaded by the divine lymph",[6] "I have only to love him and let myself be loved").[7] She prays, "that I may be ... abandoned to thy creative action ... and the Master may carry me where he will";[8] and, "Spirit of Love, come down in me, and thou, Father, deign to bend over

[3] Elizabeth de la Trinité, *Ecrits spirituels* (Ed. du Seuil, Paris), p. 17.
[4] *Ibid.*, p. 109.
[5] *Ibid.*, pp. 61, 65, 69, 72, 81, 97, 105, 106, only the verb *envahir*.
[6] *Ibid.*, p. 106.
[7] *Ibid.*, p. 73.
[8] *Ibid.*, p. 98.

this poor little creature, cover her with thy shadow";[9] and, lastly, "Master, take me, take all of me".[10]

One feels that the longer woman proceeds along the way of prayer, the more she asks for this love. She asks for it more than she promises it, because to want to be loved is her specific way of loving.

It is a yielding to love which is not simply being loved (which is a fact), but precisely *a will* to be loved (a tension), with all that it implies of opening, availability and humble submission. I have spoken of an *asceticism* of acceptance, but might with greater reason speak of a *mysticism* of acceptance (but is there a mysticism which is not that of acceptance, and an asceticism which is not also potentially mystical?).

If woman can perhaps better approach the Holy Spirit, the Holy Spirit can also approach womanly dimensions. There is, for instance, the *Veni, Sancte Spiritus*, which is clearly feminine in attitude. And, on the other hand, man's prayers are also feminine when they reach the essentially receptive mystical dimension. At this stage—at least on the level of an approach to giving—there is no longer much difference, and a woman can recognize herself fully in certain pages of the contemplatives, which unfortunately have not entered into the liturgy (perhaps, on account of their nature, they could not have done so). It is to be hoped—as has already happened with the breviary (the nocturne of the Saturday of the third week after the octave of Pentecost)—the last page of the Bible, the splendid and stupendously feminine ending of the Apocalypse will be included in the ferial lesson: "The Spirit and the Bride say, Come. Let everyone who listens answer, Come . . . come, Lord Jesus."[11]

[9] *Testamento spirituale—Ultimi ritiri Postulazione generale* (O.C.D., Rome, 1953), p. 15.
[10] *Ecrits spirituels*, p. 41.
[11] Apolcalypse 22. 17, 20.

Translated by James Langdale

Ianthe Pratt

Prayer in the Home—
A Mother's Testimony

THE development of a child's religious awareness and response to God, of which prayer is one aspect, very largely depends on the quality of Christian living experienced in the home. From the earliest years, even months, before he can consciously understand, the child senses the attitude of the parents and other children towards God.

Experience of love and security in the home is essential for his development into a mature person able to love God and neighbour generously. It is not enough that the family regularly say their prayers. They need to live by the spirit of Christ, otherwise the children will sense that the prayers are only paying lip-service to God. Parents will sometimes fail to live up to their Christian vocation. But what really matters is the children's impression of the importance they place on trying to please God. Both parents are involved in this. Too often only the mother leads the children in prayer or talks to the children about God. The father ought to share this work even if his time is limited. Otherwise, the children, and especially boys, may reject religion in later years as something domestic and feminine which has little to do with the world outside.

One of the great advantages of worship in the home is the freedom from rules and set forms. This makes it possible to adapt what one does to the needs of the children. For example, we talk about God with the children and this cannot always be separated easily from actual prayer, the one intermingles with the

other. This informality is useful for it enables thinking and praying about God and his relation with man to become part of everyday life and reflect our children's interests and activities.

We have found that a young child will readily give thanks and
praise to God for the good things in his life—his toys and games,
nice things to eat, his hands which God has given him to make
things with, his legs which God has given him to run with, his
friends, and pets. The growing wonder of the child at the world
of nature can be channelled into praise and thanksgiving not only
by making up simple prayers but by using some of the psalms.
Children brought up from the earliest years on psalms like
number 135 (136)—"Give thanks to the Lord for he is good"—
will spontaneously, from the age of three onwards, run round the
garden singing, for example, Praised is God for flowers, for but-
terflies or for the sunshine. Some psalms are particularly suitable
for children. Psalm 99, for instance, combines the ideas of joy,
of our being the Lord's own people, that we should praise and
thank him, and that his love endures for ever.

If the liturgical cycle is to have any meaning for the younger
child it needs to be brought into the home in a simplified form.
Above all we need to mark Easter as the climax of the liturgical
year. The parish ceremonies are too long for the younger children
and use language that is beyond them. The solution is to adapt
the Holy Week liturgy for use in the home.

My husband and I try to make Easter stand out for our children
as the most important feast of the year. For weeks beforehand the
children are making decorations with a liturgical motif such as
the paschal lamb or candle, and making models of the empty
tomb for the garden or house. The box in which the children
have saved their lenten alms (towards some particular project like
a tractor for use in an underdeveloped country) is given a central
place on the Easter table.

During Holy Week we have a Passover supper based on the
Jewish *Seder* brought to its fulfilment in Christ.[1] We invite as
many friends as we can fit in, together with their children, and
when we are able to have a priest with us the supper is preceded
by a simple Eucharist which incorporates the *mandatum*. We

[1] P. Rosenberg, "A Christian Passover Service", appendix to *Liturgy Is
What We Make It*, O. and I. Pratt (London, 1967).

have found it better to have hands rather than feet washed, not only to avoid difficulty with clothing but because it seems more relevant—washing feet no longer has the significance that it did in Christ's time. One advantage of a domestic *mandatum* is that everybody can be included, regardless of age or sex.

The centrepiece of the Passover supper table is the traditional *Seder* dish with its symbolic foods—the lamb bone and boiled egg representing the Temple sacrifices; the horse radish, bitter and wild herbs the suffering of the Hebrews; the *charoset* (a paste made of nuts and fruit, etc.), probably signifying the mortar used by the Hebrews in forced building labour. There are also the *matzos*, or unleavened bread; salt water representing the tears shed in exile; and wine for the cups of blessing.

The children take a central part in the service. It is they who ask the traditional questions: "Why is this night different from all other nights?", "Why do we eat lamb on this night?", and so on, to which a parent gives in reply a short account of some aspect of the exodus story which is related also to the new passover brought about by Christ. Four cups of wine (or grape juice for the children) are blessed and drunk and the prayers are interspersed with the singing of psalms and gospel songs. In the middle of the service, roast lamb is eaten. The feasting, talking and laughter interwoven with the prayers and singing provide a fruitful liturgical experience, a blend of spiritual and temporal rejoicing. We have found that children of all ages, from the very youngest to adolescents, gain a great deal from participating in such a Passover meal.

Our children are still too young to go to the parish Easter Vigil, so we hold our family ceremony on the evening of Holy Saturday with the lighting of our own paschal candle—previously decorated by the children—a short reading of the exodus story by parent or older child, and the singing of psalms of thanksgiving or praise. We then renew our baptismal promises using a simplified form, for instance we "turn away from Satan and all evil" instead of "renouncing" his "allurements".

Throughout the year we have found a family prayer meal to be very effective. Based on the early Christian *Agape* it is really an extended form of grace using the family meal as a symbol of the unity and love that Christ asked us all to show one another.

Short passages from a children's Bible are read and there are informal prayers for the needs of the family, the local community or the world, often concerning some current problem or event like a famine, or war, or a local disaster. There are also blessings of food and drink (adapted from the *Didache*) and we sing gospel or other modern religious songs. We often use the Caribbean setting of the *Our Father* with mimed gestures, and Geoffrey Beaumont's version of the *Ubi Caritas*—"There is God".[2] The verse: "Let there be no more bitter words and let quarrels stop so that Christ our God may be among us", is very relevant to the needs of children and indeed our nine-year-old son chooses this himself as his favourite bedtime prayer. We often use modern gospel songs like Malcolm Stewart's "When He Comes Back"[3] which was written especially for the World Congress of the Laity in 1967. In common with other songs of this type, it has a valuable simplicity and directness in pointing out the implications of Christianity: "By the light of our living on earth we'll discover his face. For the face of the master is always at hand: in the hungry, the poor, in the stranger—the face of a man."

Our eldest children are now seven and nine and have reached the stage where they are interested in choosing themes for prayer-meals and making up their own prayers. On one occasion they decided, after discussion, on a theme of saying "yes" to God. They drew pictures of Adam and Eve disobeying God and of Mary's "yes" at the Annunciation. The elder boy wrote a prayer about this and chose a reading from a children's Bible, picking the account of Samuel in the Temple saying, "Here I am, Lord". We made up new words for the well-known "Kumbaya" tune, asking the Lord's help to make us love him, to live at peace, to be kind to others.

These prayer-meals seem to enable children to pray with real personal involvement more effectively than night prayers which only too easily become a matter of routine. There is a place for the child's bedtime prayer—for instance, thanking God for the good things of the day and asking his forgiveness for wrong things done—but just because it is done every day, even though

[2] *Is This Your Life?*, 20th Century Church Light Music Group (London, 1967).
[3] *Gospel Song Book* (London, 1968).

one may vary the prayers, real, conscious involvement becomes less likely.

Ceremonies in the home, on the other hand, have more impact because they take place only occasionally and because they come closer to a total experience involving the whole person, for they use music, symbol, gesture and the visual arts as well as words. When they first hear about these prayer-meals, people with older children often feel it would be impossible to introduce them into a family with teenagers. One family we know, however, found that their adolescents quickly overcame their initial suspicion and reluctance. They have taken over running the *Agape* with enthusiasm and bring in their own friends.

As children become older the emphasis in family prayer has to shift more towards the practical implications of Christianity in a world full of social injustice, hunger and poverty, racialism and war. It is especially important with teenage children that worship evokes a response in the heart as well as the mind so that the whole person is involved. Folk music is particularly valuable for this purpose. Many folk songs in use today express Christian truths, for instance about brotherly love, justice and peace, in a way that is relevant to the thought, language and feeling of the young.

As the children grow older, they are likely to want to worship more with their own age group in school or youth group than with the family, but before this stage is reached it is important that the family has given them a training in participating crea-tively in worship, so that they are able to work out prayers and services as the need arises. This is something which our Christian formation has largely failed to do in the past. Although many of us are now becoming practised at making up *extempore* bidding prayers, few have reached the high standard of many members of other Churches. I have been very impressed, while taking part in local ecumenical house meetings, by the way the Methodists, in particular, are able to make up spontaneous prayers that are both reverent and relevant. If we can help our children to do this it should enrich their spiritual life and help them relate prayer and Christian living. If we are to transform the world we need to make sure that our children, who are the Christian community of the future, are able to interrelate worship and action. Either without the other is sterile.

David Power

Home or Group Prayer and the Divine Office

THE divine office is usually referred to as "the prayer of the Church". I wish to consider whether it is justifiable to speak of the prayer of the Church in this way, excluding all other forms of prayer besides the divine office. Other articles in this issue have given some idea of the actual practice of prayer among Christians. I shall try to evaluate the situation and to determine an approach to the various current forms of prayer.

I. THE DIVINE OFFICE

The early growth of the divine office was influenced by the desire to fulfil the counsel of the Lord that we ought always to pray. It was also closely connected with the commemoration of the death and resurrection of Christ. The daily office developed from three different sources: the advice given to individuals about daily prayer, the daily common prayer of the local church community, and the longer prayer sessions of ascetics and monks. Hence the present divine office incorporates responses to different prayer-needs. The idea that it is offered to God as the prayer of the Church, and in the name of the Church, is relatively recent; this is also true of the idea that certain persons, such as priests or religious, are deputed to pray the office in the name of the Church.

The problem of the reform of the divine office is that of meeting the prayer-needs of the present day. Reforms are liable to be *a priori*, and hierarchically imposed, rather than parts of a living growth, Spirit-directed, and emerging from the body of the Church. The common prayer of the Church in early days was a growth from within the body, directed by wise counsels but not rigorously structured and universally enforced. It is a mistake to approach the question of the renewal of the office on the basis of preconceived theory about what it should be, as if "the prayer of the Church" had to take a definite form. We should rather try to discern the prayer-needs of the people, meet these in a way consonant with Christian tradition yet respectful of new conditions, and then allow a theology of prayer to develop which takes account of the action of the Spirit in the Church and of changes which take place under his influence. Monks and clergy as well as the laity tend to find the office proposed as "the prayer of the Church" an alien thing.[1] New ways of praying and new modes of expression are required. That which is not prayed by the Church can scarcely be called the prayer of the Church on the basis of preconceived theories.

In his contribution to the 1961 edition of Fr Martimort's *L'Eglise en Prière* Abbot Salmon states that the layman who recites the divine office privately performs a good work but does not offer liturgical prayer. The author says that such prayer is not taken up by Christ as Head of the Mystical Body and given value through the merits of the Church.[2] To pray in the name of the Church, one must be delegated to do so by the hierarchy, and use a text approved by the same authority. Even the theology of the office found in the Vatican Council's document on the liturgy is not very different. On the one hand, it obviously wishes to see the office reinstated as the prayer of the Church community, and for this reason calls for more popular participation. On the other hand, it still gives special value to the divine office when recited by those deputed by the hierarchy, because this deputation means that they pray in the name of the Church.

Such affirmations give rise to a number of questions. Does the office recited in private or in common, by persons deputed to do so, really have a special value? Is prayer according to texts prescribed or approved by the hierarchy necessarily better than other

---

[1] Cf. *La Maison-Dieu*, no. 95 (1968), p. 141.
[2] Cf. P. Salmon, "La prière des heures", in A. Martimort, *L'Eglise en Prière* (Paris–Tournai, 1961), pp. 869–70.

prayer? Can the office in its present form, even when officially revised, again become the prayer of the Church community?

II. Group Prayer

Over against the official view of the prayer of the Church we have to consider the facts of prayer in the life of the faithful people of God. Only then can we see what the role of the institutional Church can be in guiding and directing the Church's prayer. It certainly must have a role, but is it the one that it is attempting at present?

The facts show innumerable attempts to find new ways of contact with Christ and the Father through prayer with one's brother. These attempts are usually made in family prayer or in group prayer, rather than in church. A regard and a desire for spontaneous prayer are not easily satisfied in official prayer forms. Some books on prayer depart from biblical prayer and other traditional formulas, in an effort to seek a contemporary idiom. There are new ways of using the Bible as a basis for prayer, where it is approached through reflection and discussion, and "listened to" in this way rather than as a reading proclaimed to the assembly. There is the use of symbolic actions not found in liturgical rites; the use of song and dance and visual aids as means of finding the presence of Christ in his people and making contact with one another "in the Lord". All this can be done more effectively in small groups, which are real living communities of persons drawn together by bonds of interest and concern, than in public churches where there is the hopeless realization that the people there gathered are not gathered *together*.

An attempt to evaluate the different forms of prayer requires more than an examination of their official status and sacramental structure. Their response to human needs must be considered too. A knowledge of the human needs enables one to ask how formal prayer-structures and these needs can be made to converge. Some assistance can be obtained from the sciences of sociology and psychology.[3] Membership in any community supposes that the

---

[3] Cf. F. Houtart–J. Remy, "A Survey of Sociology as applied to Pastoral Work", in *Concilium*, 3, 1, pp. 50–7 (American edn.: Vol. 3).

member has a sense of belonging and that he embraces and personalizes the values on which the community is built. Sociological and psychological investigations seem to show that smaller
groups have considerable importance in helping the individual
to relate to the larger society of which he is a member, and in the
formation of religious attitudes. Within small groups the individual learns to appreciate and assimilate values and to express
himself in relation to them. As far as religious attitudes and
membership of the Church are concerned, the individual Christian can be greatly helped in developing Christian maturity
through participation in the life and action of small groups. In
the early years of life the most important of these groups is
the family. In adolescence and youth this is complemented by the
school or club, or by apostolic groups. Even the adult needs
the aid of groups in developing his relation to society and to the
Church. As prayer is important in the formation of religious
attitudes, prayer within these groups is not only useful but even
necessary. The individual often learns to pray within these groups
rather than in church. This is especially true of children in the
family, but also true to a large extent for the other groups.
Through prayer the Christian dimension of certain groups is developed, and vital human relations are incorporated into the kingdom of God.

Bringing out the value of prayer in such mini-groups might
seem to some a devaluation of the prayer of the Church community, which is presided over by an ordained minister and conducted according to structures and formulas approved by
authority. A well-balanced view, however, would suggest that we
should follow the norm: do this and do not neglect that. Prayer
in family groups or in other small groups will in the long run
serve rather than militate against the efficacy of prayer in the
larger church congregation.

To begin with, group prayer can help towards a true appreciation of liturgical prayer and can eventually exercise some influence
upon the content of liturgical prayer. In estimating the value of
the Church's prayer and in estimating the action of God in this
prayer, the content of the prayer is just as important as the
official designation of persons or the official approval of the texts.
God is present in the gathering of two or three in Christ's name,

in the faith which they possess, in the word to which they listen, and in the groanings of the Spirit which find expression in their formulated desires. No more than one just learns to appreciate music or art can one just learn to appreciate and take part in liturgy by exposure to it. The tremendous advantage of family or another form of group prayer is that it allows for greater informality and spontaneity and thus can help the participant to learn to appreciate and value what is found in liturgy. By a combination of reading, discussion, reflection and spontaneous prayer the members of these groups learn to discover God and Christ in the Bible, in their life and in their fellow men. No liturgy is possible without this triple discovery, yet it comes to the child more readily and effectively in home life than in the church; to the adolescent in the natural groupings of that age (if they are taught to pray together); and to the adult within the intimacy of those with whom he shares some need, interest or concern. The same basic structures and content that have always been given to the liturgy can be given to group prayer, but in a more informal way. This comprises the use of the Bible as the basis of reflection and prayer, the community's expression of its admiration, thanksgiving, penitence, praise and desire, and the use of gesture and symbolic action. In the use of texts for reflection or self-expression, the Church of former days was prepared to go beyond the Bible or official forms. A certain stagnation has afflicted us in this regard. Perhaps group prayer will enable the hierarchical Church to discover the texts and symbolic actions that speak best to the people of our time in different places, and to incorporate these into the official liturgy.

The practice of group prayer must also have some influence on our idea of the nature or composition of the local Church community. It is increasingly accepted that one cannot divide the Church into basic communities founded on geographic boundaries. This is particularly true of the parish, but also to some extent of the diocese. People living in the same geographical area, especially in cities, do not form closely knit communities. Hence it is impossible to try to form them into living and working communities of persons. This implies a re-thinking of Church structures and also a re-thinking of forms of worship.

The formation of groups on a voluntary, and perhaps transient, basis, with some religious or apostolic purpose uniting them, can help the Church to find its new structures,[4] and to discover on what basis the individual Christian community ought to be founded in present-day society. Prayer within these groups is necessary to give a proper basis in God's word and power to such Christian congregations and to whatever structures may emerge from them. But larger assemblies, such as come together in public places of worship, must not be treated as if they were closely knit communities of persons intimately acquainted with one another. The worship has to unite strangers momentarily in a common worship of God, and give the participants the impression of belonging, allowing them to identify themselves with the Church. But public prayer in such large congregations, in official places of worship, seems to depend to a large extent on the apprenticeship of prayer within small groups; it would be foolish to expect people to derive the satisfaction and sense of identity from them which of their nature belong to prayer in small groups.

Two kinds of gathering for worship would seem to be necessary. First of all, there must be the gathering of the primary group, such as family, school, club, study circle, apostolic body, etc. If, however, Christians worshipped exclusively in such groups they could become introverted, self-centred, and unconcerned with the needs of the Church as a whole. Hence the larger Church gatherings are needed as well. But the two kinds of gathering respond to different needs; together they form that which in the concrete can be termed the prayer of the Church— if we understand this as the prayer which is in practice offered by the Church, and if we agree that both kinds of assembly are necessary for genuine prayer, based on a living faith, within the body of God's people.

[4] Cf. J. H. Fichter, *Social Relations in the Urban Parish* (Chicago, 1954), pp. 156–7: "...the attempt to include all lay, voluntary, parochial activity into relatively few formal artificial organizations minimizes both effectiveness (achieving purpose) and efficiency (getting people to contribute effort) ...the neglect of informal small groupings (sometimes called 'natural groups') constitutes one of the greatest social wastes in the apostolic potential of the parish."

III. Role of Church Authority

Therefore authority in the Church ought not to concern itself exclusively with public worship or with the divine office conceived as an official prayer rendered according to set texts. Authority and leadership must also give guidance to family prayer and group prayer. These form part of the prayer of the Church; and even if we wish to retain the term *divine office* as a designation of public and official worship, we must remember that the divine office originated in an attempt to give all the members of the Church a guideline for the practice and apprenticeship of prayer. In its present form it incorporates what was originally part of communal worship under the presidency of bishop, presbyter or deacon, what was more personal or private, and what was the communal prayer of non-clerical, monastic or ascetic groups. In early centuries attempts were made to meet the different needs of different categories of persons in different ways. In the present age, the efforts of families and the various primary and natural groups of our time to unite with God in prayer, and to take on the burden of the world's sufferings in the face of God, also deserve to be considered as part of the prayer of the Church. There is no good reason why only one form of prayer should be designated as the "prayer of the Church", or why the Church's authority should attend only to the promotion of the divine office as its official prayer.

The office of authority and leadership with regard to family prayer and group prayer is delicate but necessary. Its role is not to impose, but to direct, advise and sanction, thus providing an assurance of fidelity, continuity of tradition and the sense of belonging within the Church. In revising the present structures of prayer and in helping the family of God to find its forms of prayer, the hierarchy of the Church would make a serious error if it were to attend only to an official divine office with approved but rigorously determined texts, intended for use in public assemblies or by officially designated persons. Then the Church would neglect the vast majority of its members. It is just as important to help those who are trying to discover the form and content of appropriate family or group prayer. This help, of course, cannot be adequately given by a centralized authority but must be largely the concern of local hierarchies.

IV. "THE PRAYER OF THE CHURCH"

The theology of the divine office often seems to suggest that it has a special value in giving glory to God or in sanctifying man, just because it is official. The divine office is surrounded by a certain mystic aura, largely because of such phrases as "the prayer of the Church", "prayer in the name of the Church" and *"ex opere operantis ecclesiae"*, which need to be re-examined; the different forms of prayer in use must also be re-evaluated.

The prayer of the Church does not come from the approval of the hierarchy, but from the groaning of the Spirit, who gives the force and grace to address God as Father. Prayer is not of the Church because it has been officially sanctioned, but because it comes surging up from within the Church in answer to the promptings of the Spirit teaching us what we ought to pray. The official sanction is a criterion of orthodoxy, or the necessary institutionalization of a common interest. The role of authority in regulating prayer would seem to be more one of sanction and approval than of creation, whereas at present it is one of attempted creation and imposition.

What has developed under the title of the prayer of the Church in recent times is not the prayer of the Church, but a prayer of specific groups in the Church—particularly clergy and religious. Its development marks the hierarchy's concern for the prayer and holiness of these specific sectors, its anxiety to serve their devotion and to help them to respond to their vocation. Only in recent decades, and especially since Vatican II, has there been an evident desire to reinstate the office as the prayer of the Church community. The desire to reconstitute the praying community, or (where it already existed through popular devotions) to place it on firmer and more authentically Christian foundations, is laudable. By drawing from sound sources of spirituality, and in a particular way from the Bible, it is possible to contribute to a solid Christian spirituality of laity and clergy; in this sense the content of the office, particularly when revised, is of special interest. But it would be a mistake to force the faithful into strict patterns of prayer by imposing rigid universal norms, as it would also be a mistake to underestimate the value of family prayer and group prayer of a more informal nature.

To classify only the divine office as the prayer of the Church, and call everything else either public devotions or private prayer, seems rather arbitrary. The prayer of the Church incorporates a wide variety of realities; and each particular form is to be valued according to the measure of the fervour of the participants and the sacramental realization of the Church which it represents. The former is an imponderable, but under the guidance of the Spirit and with the co-operation of all the members of the Church, we must look for the forms and content of prayer which best arouse ardent and authentic Christian devotion in today's Church. As for the second, it can be had in many different degrees.

The special efficacy of any liturgical action comes from its sacramental manifestation of the mystery of Christ in his Church. Christ is present and active in the liturgy, because of the various ways in which this presence is manifested: in the gathering of two or three in his name, in his word, in the prayer of faith formulated according to the promptings of the Spirit, in the various symbolic actions which indicate personal communion with him, and in the person of the ordained minister who acts as the representative of Christ's headship. All these elements, or only some of them, can be present. Where any are present, prayer may be called the prayer of the Church. Some of them are certainly present in group and family prayer as well as in public assemblies, so that in them we have prayer which is the effect of Christ's presence in his Church, and prayer which is beneficial to his Church.

The term *"ex opere operantis ecclesiae"* is sometimes applied to the divine office to denote what is considered to be its particular efficacy. Like the term *"ex opere operato"*, however, it can only mean some particular efficacy found in the office when it is used properly; such efficacy derives from the fact that it is a fuller sacramental manifestation of the Church than group prayer, at least when it is a genuine community prayer. Its special intercessory value comes from the fact that it is a special manifestation of God's salvific will, involving the new creation of the believing community in a special way. The need of the individual to take part in such prayer is the need for him to make a personal appropriation of the faith of the Church, and to experience and assent to membership of the Church community. Like participation in the sacraments, however, it is of little value unless the participant is conscious, devoted and generous.

At present, when priests or religious are said to pray in the name of the Church, their prayer is supposed to have some special significance for the Church. But the term "in the name of" was chosen to avoid "in the person of", and originated in a juridical context of no particular theological significance, simply as a way of explaining the obligation to recite the divine office imposed on these persons.[5] The imposition of the office on priests and religious ought really to be seen as a way of assuring that they respond to their vocation, which certainly includes a call to a more devoted prayer. The charismatic call, however, and the answer to it, not the official designation to pray, are of value to the Church. Without the grace, charity and fervour of the persons praying, this prayer is of no particular value.[6] The meaning of the official mandate needs to be sought in the order of sign; it is the institution's way of indicating the effort to assure the presence in the Church community of persons who do pray more often and more fervently for the Church, in answer to a special call of grace. It is a way of constituting clerics and religious as signs or witnesses of the Church's dependence on and union with its head, Jesus Christ. As a prophetic sign and a provocation to the other members of the Church, the prayer of such persons can be of value and has its official place in the Church, just as in early centuries the prayer of the order of widows and virgins was given

[5] Cf. B.-D. Marliangeas, " 'In persona Christi', 'In persona Ecclesiae'. 'Note sur les origines et le développement de l'usage de ces expressions dans la théologie latine", in J.-P. Jossua-Y. Congar, *La Liturgie après Vatican II* (Paris, 1967), *Unam Sanctam*, 66, pp. 283–8.

[6] Cf. A. Häussling, art. "Breviary", in *Sacramentum Mundi*, 1 (London and New York, 1968), p. 238: "Just as frequent reception of the sacraments does not automatically increase grace and give still more glory to God if not accompanied by a profounder dedication in faith, so too the Breviary is not 'better' just because it is the 'prayer of the Church' and is performed by 'official mandate'. It is only (and always) better when it is a sign of profounder dedication to the Lord...."

its public character and its place in Church order.[7] The prescription of special prayer texts is the authority's way of assuring that the vocation receives its proper and fitting response; like all norms, those whereby prescribed texts and forms are laid down ought to be flexible; otherwise they may not achieve their intended purpose, namely the fervent and beneficial prayer of those to whom they are given.

IV. The Sanctification of Time

The Vatican constitution on the liturgy also speaks of the divine office as a sanctification of time, and for this reason prescribes that due attention be given to saying the different canonical hours at their appropriate times. But the rhythm envisaged by the office is the natural rhythm of the day. How genuine can this be in an age when man ignores natural rhythms only to impose his own according to the needs of his work?

The practice of daily prayer, and the use of the divine office as the daily prayer of the Christian assembly, cannot be separated from the question of a daily celebration of the Eucharist. The early growth of the office came about at a time when this was not customary, so that the community's daily prayer was in fact not the Mass but the office. Nowadays, family prayer and group prayer are more likely to be the daily, or at least week-day (for it may not be daily) prayer of so many people than the Mass or the office. Those who are accustomed to the daily recitation of the office are the special groups, namely clergy and religious, who are also accustomed to daily Mass.

Is it realistic to try to reinstate the divine office as the prayer of the Church community in public assembly alongside the Eucharist as a daily gathering? Should we allow the Mass to be accepted as the one daily prayer gathering in public places of worship, or should we admit that because prayer, including that of the Mass, depends so much on the faith of the participants, on some days it would be preferable to have the common prayer of Matins or Vespers rather than Mass? This latter practice would be in keeping with the necessary emphasis on the faith of those taking part in the liturgy, and on the need to arouse and educate

[7] Cf., e.g., Hippolytus of Rome, *The Apostolic Tradition*, ed. G. Dix–H. Chadwick (London, 1968), pp. 20-1.

it in many and varied ways. But whatever may be done about the daily assembly in public places of worship, whether for Mass or for the office, it is likely that family prayer and group prayer will retain a greater practical importance in the lives of most people than any such assembly. These forms of prayer constitute a large part of the "prayer of the Church"; therefore, it is to be hoped that they will receive adequate attention from the pastoral guidance of the Church's ordained ministers.

Robert Ledogar

Table Prayers and Eucharist: Questions from the Social Sciences

EVERYONE says that liturgy should be more open to social sciences. Clearly that is one direction that liturgical studies must take in the future. *Concilium* is the kind of review which should lead the way in this new direction.

But the problems are so vast. Mastery of all that has been written on the Eucharist from the historical and theological perspectives alone is a full-time job. Inter-disciplinary studies require knowledge of several new sciences, and a special methodology needs to be elaborated. Teamwork is called for, but finding a common terminology and classification is difficult.

The subject of table prayers, however, is small enough and central enough to provide a focus for considering some of the problems entailed.

The following is the effort of one trained in theology and liturgical history to consider a liturgical question in the light of certain bits of information that he, as a non-specialist in these fields, has uncovered in the writings of sociologists and anthropologists. Inevitably these latter are mostly American.

I. THE THEOLOGICAL IMPORTANCE OF TABLE PRAYERS

It would be difficult to exaggerate the importance of table prayers for the theology of the Eucharist. Or, better perhaps, it would be difficult to exaggerate the importance of a religious attitude towards food as expressed traditionally in the custom of meal prayers. It has become quite clear to modern theology that none of the sacraments can be considered in isolation from the human realities that are the source of their meaning as signs. Anointing of the sick cannot be considered in isolation from the significance of illness in human life; the sacrament of matrimony cannot be considered in isolation from the entire context of the human institutions called marriage and the family or from the events of encounter and interpersonal communion. The sacraments are human realities which already have "signification" prior to their having become Christians signs of salvation.[1]

Not only is the Eucharist a thanksgiving meal and a thanksgiving sacrifice, it presupposes an attitude of thank-offering as its point of departure. The Eucharist is not primarily an act of thanksgiving to God for all the good things of life and creation. It takes that for granted and moves beyond to a celebration of salvation in a distinctively eschatological perspective.

But the entire tradition of the eucharistic prayer is built up around the understanding that the bread and wine offered for the sacrifice are already symbols prior to their becoming the body and blood of the Lord. They are already gifts of God and they are chosen *de suis donis ac datis*. "We offer him that which is his", said Irenaeus,[2] and the eucharistic prayer of St John Chrysostom concludes its *anamnesis* with similar words—"offering to you gifts which are already your gifts to us, we praise you. . . ."[3]

When Paul, in 1 Corinthians 10. 16, speaks of the Eucharist as *koinonia* in the body and blood of Christ, it is clear from the context that a loaf and a cup are already signs of *koinonia* prior to their specifically Christian reference. Even those modern theologies which speak of eucharistic "transsignification" are predicated on the notion that bread and wine already have a signification to begin with.

A religious attitude towards food, then, is quite fundamental to the theology of the Eucharist. Such a religious attitude is absorbed, not only at the Eucharist itself but in the day to day receiving of food. Where food is a sign of fellowship and

---

[1] Cf. E. Schillebeeckx, *Marriage: Secular Reality and Saving Mystery*, 2 Vols. (London, 1965).

[2] *Adv. Haer.*, IV, 31, 3 (ed. Harvey, II, p. 203).

[3] F. E. Brightman, *Liturgies Eastern and Western, Vol. I: Eastern Liturgies* (Oxford, 1896), p. 329.

participation in the mystery of life, where ordinary food is acknowledged as a gift from God the author of life, there we have the
traditional context for the Christian Eucharist. Whenever such
a context was forgotten the Eucharist has stood isolated, it lost
its relation to daily life and easily took on the aspect of a magical
rite.

II. THE HISTORICAL IMPORTANCE OF TABLE PRAYERS IN CHRISTIANITY

Historically, the importance of table prayers in Christianity
comes from the fact that the Eucharist was originally celebrated
in the context of a meal. Curiously enough, ordinary meals and
meal prayers seem to take on greater historical importance if one
chooses to follow the more radical New Testament critics on
the subject of eucharistic origins. If the Eucharist is linked very
closely to the Jewish Passover meal, following J. Jeremias,[4] then
the setting is a very specialized one (though not without deep
significance for the religious interpretation of all meals). If the
Eucharist is considered more in the context of a festive meal as
distinct from an "everyday meal" (H. Schurmann[5]), the relationship of everyday eating to the eating of the Lord's supper is
more obvious.

But if one follows the more radical critics who say that early
Christianity did not clearly distinguish between a meal shared
among disciples of the Lord and a special commemoration of the
Last Supper incorporating the words of institution,[6] then attention naturally focuses more readily on the whole context of meals
and meal prayers in primitive Christianity, in the Judaism of
Jesus' time, and in the Hellenistic world.

Whatever their tendencies in this regard, exegetes generally

[4] J. Jeremias, *The Eucharistic Words of Jesus* (New York, 1966).
[5] H. Schürmann, "Jesus' Words in the Light of His Actions at the Last
Supper", in *Concilium*, 40 (1969); British edition, December 1968.
[6] E. Schweitzer, *The Lord's Supper: According to the New Testament*
(Philadelphia, 1967) (a translation, revised and edited of the article Abend-
mahl I in *Die Religion in Geschichte und Gegenwart*, 3rd edn., Vol. I,
pp. 10–21); R. D. Richardson, Supplementary Essay to H. Lietzmann, *Mass
and Lord's Supper* (Leiden, no date, publication still in progress), fascicle
5, pp. 221 ff.

see some eucharistic significance in many of the meals described or mentioned in the New Testament other than the Lord's farewell supper, and especially the eating that is a feature of the Resurrection accounts.[7]

Historians of the primitive Church and of the early liturgy have been led by greater interest in the literary or cultic form of the eucharistic prayer to investigate the religious significance of meals and meal prayers in Judaism.[8] The praise and thanksgiving theme which dominates the eucharistic prayer in all liturgies has been shown to originate in some form of Jewish berakah pronounced over bread and wine at a Jewish meal.[9]

The gradual separation of the Eucharist from its primitive meal context is a phenomenon about which we know very little. Although it was certainly accomplished in the Roman community described by Justin in the middle of the second century,[10] the separation was perhaps neither total nor universal at that time.[11] At the close of that century we see a distinct type of religious fellowship meal which is not eucharistic described by Hippolytus in Rome and Tertullian in Africa.[12] This is the meal known as the agape which seems still to have been a living, if perhaps occasional, institution in fourth-century Alexandria.[13] Traces of it are found even later than this.[14]

Religious meals were frequently held by Christians before the fifth century in connection with funerals and anniversaries of the dead, as archaeological, pictorial and literary evidence attests.[15] The relationship of the Eucharist celebrated in memory of the

---

[7] For Luke see references in The Jerome Biblical Commentary, ed. R. E. Brown et al. (Englewood, N.J., 1968; London, 1969), section 44. No. 177.

[8] Cf. L. Bouyer, Eucharist (Univ. of Notre Dame Press, 1968).

[9] J. P. Audet, La Didachè, Instructions des Apôtres (Paris, 1958), pp. 375–387.

[10] Apologia, 1, 67 (J. Quasten, Monumenta Eucharistica et Liturgica Vetustissima, Bonn, 1935, p. 19).

[11] Cf. Epistula Apostolorum (Quasten, p. 337).

[12] Tertullian, Apologeticum, 39 (Corpus Christianorum, I, pp. 150–3); Hippolytus, Apostolic Tradition, 25, 28, ed. Botte (Münster, 1963), pp. 64–73.

[13] R. Coquin, Les Canons d'Hippolyte, Patrologia Orientalis, xxxi, 2 (Paris, 1966), pp. 402–9.

[14] Cf. H. Lietzmann, Das Sakramentarium Gregorianum, Liturgiegesch. Quellen. und Forschungen, 3 (Münster, 1921), p. 126, no. 210.

[15] See the dictionaries and encyclopedias under "Refrigerium".

dead (especially the early martyrs) to this *refrigerium*, or funeral banquet, is not entirely clear. If it is a mistake to depict them as originally inseparable, it is also a mistake to consider them in isolation from each other.

Many examples of a eucharistic reference in the table prayers of religious communities in the East are provided by E. von der Goltz in a fundamental study of this whole question.[16] Bread that is blessed and called *eulogia* has had a significant place in Christian piety. It seems to have been quite a common practice for bishops at the turn of the fifth century to exchange gifts of blessed bread (in an earlier time they exchanged the Eucharist itself[17]) as a symbol of their union with each other.[18] The practice of distributing blessed bread to those who do not take the Eucharist at the Sunday liturgy lasted well into the Middle Ages in the West and continues to this day in the East.[19]

While we know almost nothing about the specific customs of the "nuclear" family as regards table prayers in early Christianity, it can be seen that the sacrament of the Lord's supper was born in a culture where, if every meal was not a deeply religious event, it could easily become so. Bread and wine were already sacred things, prior to their becoming the body and blood of the Lord, for "everything that God created is good, and nothing is to be rejected when it is taken with thanksgiving, since it is hallowed by God's own word and by prayer" (1 Tim. 4. 4).

III. The Importance of Meal Prayers in Contemporary Christianity

As other sections of this volume show, it is necessary for the "official" liturgy to be more closely related to the prayer life of different kinds of Christian families. A liturgical renewal which emphasizes only the official Eucharist and which is not supported by a renewal in the prayer life of Christians at all levels and in

[16] E. von der Goltz, *Tischgebete und Abendmahlsgebete in der altchristlichen und in der griechischen Kirche*, Texte und Untersuchungen, N.F. 14, 2b (Leipzig, 1905).

[17] Eusebius, *Hist. Eccl.*, V, 24, 15; *P.G.*, 20, 505.

[18] A. Franz, *Die Kirchlichen Benedektionen im Mittelalter* (Freiburg im Breisgau, 1909), vol. I, p. 240.

[19] *Ibid.*, pp. 229–78.

all circumstances is little more than a shifting of furniture. Although the classic model on which our eucharistic liturgy is based is an assembly of many and divergent families "of every race and people and tongue", each of these families must bring to that assembly a sense and tradition of prayer, and especially thanksgiving, if they are truly to participate and not simply be spectators.

The reform of the Roman liturgy that has taken place so far has largely been a restoration of the liturgy to the simplicity of a time when it was truly vital and able to nourish and sustain the faith of people in high station and low. Such a liturgy evidently presupposes some of the cultural and religious attitudes of that time. If such attitudes have been lost in our own time the meaning of the liturgical rites, perfectly valid in themselves, may be lost to our contemporaries.

IV. Problems Raised by Sociology

Some statistical studies have been conducted on the frequency of table prayers in American family life. Meal prayers, like family devotions in general, seem to be more frequent in Protestant families than among Catholics (at least when the Catholics are of Irish extraction).[20] Of all the possible forms of family devotion, "grace at meals" tends to disappear more slowly,[21] but it is frequently something which only the children do, and, if the trends of the past forty to fifty years continue, it faces the same future as all other forms of family prayer.[22]

It is interesting to note that family prayer has been the object of a constant and faithful catechesis on the part of Protestant clergymen and educators. Fairchild and Wynn wrote in 1961:

> The one family subject that receives more pulpit attention than any other is family worship. This traditional ideal of Protestant

[20] J. Bossard and E. Boll, *Ritual in Family Living: A Contemporary Study* (Philadelphia, 1950), p. 120; cf. P. D'Arcy, *Factual Differences between the Sexes in the Field of Religion*, unpublished dissertation (Catholic University of America, 1947).

[21] R. W. Fairchild and J. C. Wynn, *Families in the Church: A Protestant Survey* (New York, 1961), pp. 184 ff.; O. E. Klapp, "Ritual and Family Solidarity", in *Social Forces*, 37 (March 1959), pp. 212–14.

[22] Fairchild and Wynn, *op. cit.*, p. 184.

families gathered together for Christian worship has been handed down from generation to generation in sermons and Church literature. . . . Extolled in thousands of magazine articles, sermons, and references every year, regular worship in the home was seldom found among the families we surveyed. . . . A few candid parents say outright what others may feel: that they are not especially interested in the practice nor convinced of its helpfulness.[23]

A study of Lutheran youth in the United States conducted between 1958 and 1962 showed that church leaders and youth workers rated "emphasis on family devotions in every home" very high in the category of "help we can give" and "help we are giving". But the same rated quite low among the youth themselves in the category of "help we want".

Obviously there is a good deal of resistance to catechesis on this subject in American Protestantism. It is hardly rash to suggest that the same might well be true of Catholics, both in North America and in other continents.

This decline of formal prayer in American family life, however, does not mean that there has been a decline in ritual activity. A remarkable study by Bossard and Boll, entitled *Ritual in Family Living*, was conducted in the region of Philadelphia and published in 1950. Although the sociological configuration of that region has changed a good deal in the ensuing twenty years, many of its findings are still highly relevant to our inquiry. Among other things, they studied the pattern of ritual activity in one family through three generations and compiled a list of factors which would tend to favour the survival of ritual in family life, and another list of things which would cause rituals to disappear.[24] Anyone presparing a collection of family prayers and religious customs for the home would do well to consult such a list.

This and similar studies also make one aware that social class, family size and level of income make a great difference as regards the importance given to food in the totality of life[25] and the degree to which the table is a true gathering place for the family. "In

[23] *Ibid*.
[24] Bossard and Boll, *op. cit.*, p. 186.
[25] F. I. Nye and F. M. Berardo, *Emerging Conceptual Frameworks in Family Analysis* (New York, 1966), pp. 250-1.

the lower-class family . . . the mother, or an older sister, does pre-pare the food, but the rest of the family comes and takes it when and where they want to. Some of these families never have a meal sitting down with the whole family together except for Sunday dinner. . . . Even at this meal some families have to eat in relays, or in different rooms, because there is not room enough for all of them at table."[26]

Given such conditions it is not surprising to read further on that "It is the middle-class families here described that carry the torch of religion in the home. . . . Grace is frequently said at meals, and in many different forms."[27] Interestingly enough, table prayers were found to be almost absent in the lives of upper-class families (*haute bourgeoisie*) where other rituals of mealtime are quite strictly observed.

The most significant conclusion of this study, however, is that while ritual activity in American family life is a continuing reality and may even be on the increase in terms of individual rituals, the process of secularization has developed at a rapid pace. Ritual is not disappearing. Religious ritual is, and it is being re-placed by secular rituals.[28] An interesting example of this process of secularization on the level of popular literature can be found in a *Reader's Digest* article which first appeared there in 1940 and was reprinted in 1963. It is entitled "Grace at Table" but it uses the word grace in the broader sense of "graciousness" and says, at one point, "The meaning of the blessing can be pre-served even without the saying of a formal grace—if only we will bring grace to the table, and be our best selves, not our pettiest, in the company of friends and family."[29]

Sociologists see that ritual can play an important part in keep-ing families together.[30] Where the rituals are in fact religious they will tend to favour their retention,[31] but one has the

---

[26] Bossard and Boll, *op. cit.*, p. 116.

[27] *Ibid.*, p. 120.

[28] *Ibid.*, p. 26.

[29] J. Richards, "Grace at Table", in *Reader's Digest,* 83 (August, 1963), p. 116.

[30] O. E. Klapp, *op. cit.*

[31] Cf. a series of articles on Ritual by K. Lorenz, J. Huxley, E. H. Erick-son, E. Shils, W. F. Lynch, *et al.*, in *The Religious Situation: 1968* (Boston, 1968), pp. 695–765.

impression that this sociological validation of ritual has very little to do *per se* with the religious content.

V. Problems Raised by Anthropology

At first glance it would appear that anthropologists are more positively interested in the religious significance of food and the ritual which surrounds the consumption of food. They also remind us that "Food is actually a different object to the hungry, and to the full man".[32] In the so-called "primitive societies" where it is scarce, food naturally becomes the focus of individual and family life and easily takes on a sacred significance. It is also a symbol of union between men.

Indeed, if any generalization is valid in this field, it seems safe to say that food in human society is not just an object of consumption, it is also a symbolic reality. Y. A. Cohen has delineated four types of human society according to the attitude of willingness to share or not share food. He concludes: "The evidence is conclusive that patterns in the consumption of food are almost always governed by cultural symbols and that the ways in which food is distributed and consumed reflect a society's dominant modes of social relationships and groupings, especially those pertaining to kinship ties.[33]

This does not mean, of course, that it is normal in all societies for all members of a family to sit down to the table together. But it does mean that the Eucharist-as-food has a solid basis for reference as a sign of human solidarity.

With his appetite whetted by such considerations, the liturgist is ready to plunge into the study of anthropology. He discovers that there is an entire division of anthropology called "culinary" to which some people wish to devote a distinct periodical.[34] Exploring the bibliography he finds an article entitled "Food Rites" by R. R. Marrett and reads:

[32] A. I. Richards, *Hunger and Work in a Savage Tribe*, Meridian Paperback edition (originally published in England 1932), 1964, p. 14.

[33] Y. A. Cohen, "Food: Consumption Patterns", in *International Encyclopedia of the Social Sciences* (New York, 1968), vol. 5, p. 513.

[34] Cf. R. L. Freedman, "Wanted: A Journal in Culinary Anthropology", in *Current Anthropology*, 9 (Feb. 1968), pp. 62 ff.

At-one-ness... is by no means the same thing as one-ness. It stands for a transcendent duality rather than for a unity that is such by nature. So, too, then, I suggest that the so-called communal food rite is from its first inception intended to effect a miracle of at-one-ment—to build a supernatural bridge across a natural divide.[35]

... in origin the sacramental meal is essentially distinct from the festal, even if later religious practice sometimes tends to confuse them.[36]

Obviously such statements offer a great deal of interest to the theologian in his effort to analyse the historical relationship of the Eucharist to ordinary meals. This passage seems to shed a particular light on how and why the Eucharist was separated from its primitive meal context, and it offers considerations for those who would restore the relationship of Eucharist to meals, especially in a home context.

But then one goes to a manual of anthropology and looks up the name of R. R. Marrett. Marvin Harris says of him: "Marrett attempted to correct for the over-intellectualized approach of Tylor and Frazer by insisting (without benefits of fieldwork) that primitives distinguish emotionally between supernatural and ordinary phenomena.... Like Frazer, Marrett stands on the boundary between the scientist and man of letters."[37]

One begins to realize that the problem here is not a brand new one. It is one that theologians struggled with a generation ago when trying to explain how the Mass is a "sacrifice". They went to Comparative Religion to look for definitions of sacrifice only to find that (1) the experts did not agree; (2) Christianity claims to have transcended the very conceptions on which any such definition would rest. Marrett develops his distinction between a sacramental meal and a festal meal on the basis of taboo and "holy fear". The Christian theologian must insist that Jesus came to destroy all that. The many gospel scenes, especially the eating scenes after the Resurrection in Luke and John, have about them

[35] R. R. Marrett, "Food Rites", *Essays Presented to C. G. Seligman*, edited by E. E. Evans-Pritchard *et al.* (London, 1934), p. 205.

[36] *Ibid.*, p. 207.

[37] M. Harris, *The Rise of Anthropological Theory: A History of Theories of Culture* (New York, 1968), p. 205.

a familiarity and a naturalness which seem so opposed to the fear-dominated religion of so-called primitive societies.

VI. RESPONSE OF THEOLOGY

The theologian is thus confronted, by both sociology and anthropology, with the problem of the sacred. The sociologist tells him that in the matter of family ritual in general and meal prayers in particular the process of desacralization is progressing at a rapid pace in Western society. The anthropologist gives him a longer historical perspective on the process of desacralization. He reminds the theologian that this process is partly a phenomenon of European and American society, not necessarily inevitable everywhere. The anthropologist also reminds the theologian, indirectly, that Christianity is deeply implicated in the process of desacralization. The Christian missionary who deals with the problem of hunger in rural Africa or Asia by promoting better fertilizer rather than by special prayer-ceremonies is an agent of desacralization. If his people are less inclined to give thanks to God for the food they eat he has chiefly himself to blame.

A Christian theology has neither the right to blame the phenomenon of secularization on some anti-Christian force, nor the right to embrace everything secular as "holy" without exercising a bit of prophetic criticism.

It seems clear that food is not about to be deprived of all symbolic value by modern society. It can still quite easily be a sign of human solidarity. If lunch counters and the automatic food dispensing machines of our urban society threaten to deprive the noonday meal of all community sense, dinner at home or in a restaurant is still very much something to share, something during which men communicate—if they do so at all.

But food as a gift from God—for which we give thanks—that is a more difficult problem. How can the city dweller or the worker on a mechanized farm offer thanks to God for food that has been fertilized, cultivated, planted and harvested mechanically, shielded by plastic coverings in the field and protected by plastic wrappers in the store? How can man, whose very survival depends upon the hope that human ingenuity will discover ways to multiply the world's agricultural yield sevenfold—how can he look at bread with a sense of gratitude for divine providence?

There is something disturbing in acts of thanks to God offered by any man who has more to eat than his neighbour, just as there is something disturbing when American public officials piously sing the praises of Providence for the fact that we have more to eat than the rest of the world.

Could it be that we must abandon the words of the Psalmist, "Let thanksgiving be your sacrifice to God" (Ps. 50. 14), and go back to the words of the prophet, "I hate and despise your feast. . . . Let justice flow like water, and integrity like an unfailing stream" (Amos 5. 21–4)?

In fact, the primitive biblical notion of thanksgiving is an act of commitment to the truth. It comes from a sense that the true source of all one has must be acknowledged. Whatever is not mine (i.e., everything) must be publicly admitted to be either a gift or stolen goods (cf. Joshua 7. 19). The very same sense of a duty to "confess" publicly the praise of Yahweh as the source of all good things is the motive for "confessing" when a man has taken something which doesn't belong to him. The same Jewish-Christian word *exhomologeisthai* is behind both ideas. To thank God for food that is stolen from the poor would be recognized by everyone as a monstrous hypocrisy. We would all expect the thief to have the simple decency to be silent.

Perhaps the reluctance of Western man, and of American Christians in particular, to "say grace" at meals stems from a latent sense of honesty. Somehow in the depth of his conscience he perceives that the food he is eating is neither a personal gift of God to him nor a purely "neutral" secular reality. It is something bought with a purchasing power that he has and others do not. He has the decency not to thank God for his purchasing power because it is not at all clear that such a power is God-given.

The theological answer, then, to the sociologist's data concerning the decline of meal prayers in Christian homes might well be to suggest that beneath the phenomenon of secularization is a deeper human problem of a society's "guilty conscience".

In the Eucharist we can all continue to thank God for the hope of human reconciliation (with redress of injustice) promised us in the resurrection of Jesus. But doing so on the basis of thanks-giving for food is going to be more and more difficult unless that thanksgiving can be turned into what it should be: confession of the truth.

Perhaps we will not have so much trouble thanking God for food, even synthetic food made by man, on the day that it is equitably distributed around our planet.

PART II
BULLETIN

Prayer and Song in the Human Family Today

Note

THE general survey (3) is preceded by some information about the practice of prayer in Italy (1) and in Ireland (2) because the practice there has had a wider influence in the world at large through emigration. Something similar should have been possible for Spain and Portugal in connection with Latin America, but because of the complexity of the subject in these two countries, it proved impossible to obtain suitable contributions.

1. Domenico Bilotti

Prayer and Song in the Human Family Today (Italy)

THE TERM "family" is not used here solely in the sense of a number of people joined by a blood relationship, but also to mean a group, assembly and community (even vast in size) having the same faith and baptism, and professing the same loyalty, albeit in varying degrees, to Christ and the Church. "Prayer" is also allowed a wider meaning. The term "liturgy" is extended from acts of worship to comprise any action or prayer.

The liturgical experience is not the whole, or the larger part of Christian life or ecclesial activity; it is an important part, and also an obligation and characteristic sign for the individual Christian and the life of the community. But it is not of definitive and absolute importance. We may say with Vatican II, *culmen et fons*, because there is no summit without a base, the source which is not followed by the stream is dry. In the Christian community, there is no specific competency or particular delegation of the new People of God to worship, which is detached from or in any way independent of life. Life itself takes on significance as worship; and all the realizations, manifestations and achievements of Christian existence are themselves priestly.

This gives us a basic rule by which to judge the relations between popular prayer-piety and liturgy, and also indicates how they may be integrated. Popular prayer-piety which degenerates into a lower form of folk-culture, or which is only "devotion" but not an expression or inspiration of Christian life in individuals or in the community, cannot be integrated into the liturgy; and there is no guarantee that it has any value or function for Christian people. Liturgy which delights in ecclesiastical ritualism, and which retains archaic formulas without communicating with Christian people, is incapable of accepting and assimilating the worthwhile content and the forms of expression of popular prayer-piety. They can meet in order to complete, enrich and integrate one another in the concrete existence of modern man. At this level one must judge their capacity to offer the faithful encouragement, motives, suggestions, expressive forms, and common motives, modes of procedure, both in content and methods, so that they may become vividly and actively conscious of the reality of baptism.[1]

Does the Italian family live and effectively practise this type of religiosity? A precise and exhaustive assessment is impossible because of the complete absence of any studies on the subject and the limitations of experience. Nevertheless, the evidence regarding the religiosity of the family of modern man in Italy provided by nation-wide statistical surveys, and—more often—those restricted to regions, dioceses, parishes, together with numerous publications on general aspects of the problem, open up wide prospects which touch on some aspects of our problem.[2]

Most people think of prayer as what is recited in church, thus making a break in human existence between daily life, work, employment, profession and spiritual life—which is relegated to the cold anonymity of a sacred space. This is the result of a formalistic and empty teaching on the one hand, and passive receptivity on the other. A definite improvement was brought about by the liturgical movement, particularly after Vatican II.

Increasingly numerous groups gather together in prayer. Their prayers are enriched by the contribution of each individual; they are live and active not only internally, but result in generous impulses, and inform and characterize the life and the activity of each person.

Within the family nucleus itself, various though consistent initiatives with regard to religious prayer are beginning to take

[1] L. Della Tore, "Liturgia e pieta popolare", in *Studi Cattolica*, 89–90 (1968), pp. 587–94.
[2] S. Burgalassi, *Italiani in Chiesa* (Brescia 1967). Particular attention is drawn to the bibliography, pp. 221–30.

shape. The anniversary of baptism is celebrated religiously: a candle received as a gift on the day of the celebration is lit, and the event is commemorated by active participation in Mass and Communion. First Communion and Confirmation are celebrated in an atmosphere of deeper prayer in which all feel committed and participate with greater fervour.

Other very significant customs are becoming established, such as the wreath with four candles during Advent. The crib belongs to folklore, but it serves as a focus for the entire family, who recite an informal but heartfelt prayer. For the very young, it is a novelty which allows them initiation into the development of religious feeling.

Above all, the word of God in the Bible is beginning to be understood and to penetrate into the soul of modern man. In several families, a page of the Bible is read and discussed before the evening meal. Prayers before and after meals, at home or in restaurants, are rarely said. The prayer which parents recite with their children before bedtime is praiseworthy.

The dead are still buried in a pious and prayerful atmosphere. When the deceased does not die at home, he is taken there from the hospital mortuary to receive the last farewell before being taken to church. Here, more often than not, one notices a sharp contrast between the serene and orderly piety at home and the hasty, agitated and incomprehensible rite that takes place in church.

The blessing of the home is a ceremony which is becoming one of pious prayer with a real liturgy of the word and sometimes even of the Eucharist. But what is happening to the family Rosary? In some isolated sectors, mostly consisting of very old people, it is still said. This is hardly surprising, as in the few churches in which it is retained, it is recited almost as a stop-gap and in Latin.

Culture seems more appreciative of the problems of family prayer. Publications of Italian authors, such as *Il breviario dei laici* (The Breviary of the Laity),[3] *Il Guastafeste* (The Spoil-Sport),[4]

---

[3] L. Rusca, *Il breviario dei laici* (Milan, 1963).
[4] A. Pronzato, *Il Guastafeste* (Turin, 1968).

Alzo zero,[5] *Prima che il gallo canti* (Before the Cock Crows),[6] *La preghiera nella poesia italiana* (Prayer in Italian Poetry),[7] *La poesia dei cattolici italiani, 1908–1968* (Italian Catholic Poetry, 1908–1968),[8] *Cuore d'uomo—Cuore di Dio* (Heart of Man—Heart of God),[9] *Osiamo dire* (We Dare to Say),[10] *Come e grande il tuo nome su tutta la terra* (How Great is Thy Name over the Whole World)[11] have obtained a wide circulation. Translations of foreign publications have been no less popular. The principal ones are *Dio e Co: Preghiera di un laico renitente* (God and Co.: The Prayer of a Reluctant Layman),[12] *Tutti i figli di Dio hanno le ali* (All the Children of God have Wings),[13] *Preghiere dell' uomo nuovo* (Prayers of the New Man),[14] *Tu sei un amico difficile* (You are a Difficult Friend).[15] In each one of the publications there are numerous other directions and recommendations.

The Italian Broadcasting and Television Services offer a valuable contribution to the spread of religious education by varied and praiseworthy programmes on the gospels, the broadcasting of Masses and sermons, reports on religious events, and on activities with a religious background and content.

Generally, however, the situation is still far from satisfactory, as the above initiatives only affect a small part of the family of modern man. But they can be put into practice, and will eventually give a new look to society.

More difficult to explain is the present position of singing. In Italy, which has a strong tradition of singing, music-lovers and world-famous composers, there is very little religious singing. In church, the congregation sings with difficulty; at home, not at

---

[5] M. Tosco, *Alzo zero* (Turin, 1968).
[6] T. Manfredi, *Prima che il gallo canti* (Rome, 1968).
[7] V. Volpini, *La preghiera nella poesia italiana* (Catania, 1969).
[8] M. Ufreduzzi, *La poesia dei cattolici italiani 1908–1968* (Rome, 1969).
[9] L. Rosadoni, *Cuore d'uomo—Cuore di Dio* (Turin, 1968).
[10] F. Barbero, *Osiamo dire* (Turin, 1968).
[11] A. M. Auxilia, *Come e grande il tuo nome su tutta la terra* (Turin, 1967).
[12] A. Muller-Felsenburg, *Dio e Co—Preghiera di un laico renitente* (Assisi, 1969).
[13] Quoist–Lebret–C. Lopez–Lelotte, *Tutti i figli di Dio hanno le ali* (Turin, 1966).
[14] F. C. Lopez, *Preghiere dell'uomo nuovo* (Rome, 1964).
[15] H. Oosterhuis, *Tu sei un amico difficile* (Assisi, 1968).

all. We are heirs to a rich tradition of polyphony, the impeccable performance of which was the privilege of a few; and the composers have devoted the best of their genius to a repertory of material in a dead and incomprehensible language.

Renewal is evident in spite of all obstacles. The LDC booklets, the ECAS cards and the new works of D. and G. Stefani, L. Picchi, E. Costa and the "beat" Masses of M. Giombini deserve mention. A more complete picture will be found in "Does the liturgy still need music?" by G. Stefani and "Jazz and folk music in the liturgy?" by H. Hucke, both in *Concilium*, 2 (1969); U.S. volume 42.

In conclusion, one might say that the family of modern man prays little and sings even less. The inadequate religious sensibility in church is not surprising, as the spirit of prayer is not cultivated or developed at home, and even less at school. It is not easy, for instance, to understand the symbolism of the eucharistic meal if modern man does not see a reality expressive of prayer in the eating of his daily meals. I hope these notes will prove a useful introduction and encouragement for the future.

Translated by James Langdale

2. Diarmuid O'Laoghaire

Prayer and Song in the Human Family Today (Ireland)

IN WRITING of this subject with regard to Ireland, even in what is but a brief note, we must realize that only recently was the Irish language replaced in many parts of the country by English and that in some areas Irish is still the vernacular. This is not an irrelevant fact, for it was in the Irish language that the faith, and the traditions attached thereto, were moulded to a distinctive Irish image. To mention but one facet of those traditions, there has come down to our day in Irish a great, and I believe, unique corpus of traditional prayer, much of which has roots in the universal prayer of the Church and is largely family prayer. In expression it is for the most part corporate, either explicitly or implicitly. There are prayers for all classes and for every occasion, Mass prayers, prayers to the Father, Son and Holy Ghost, to Our Lady, the great saints of the Church and the native saints. The Blessed Trinity is constantly called on.

Very little of that heritage of prayer found its way into English. Hence the prayers and songs we speak of, outside the Irish-speaking areas, differ very little from those of what is called the English-speaking world. So it is that one might dismiss in a couple of sentences the matter of religious song in most of Ireland: "It would be no exaggeration to say that one could count on the fingers of two hands the number of hymns which are commonly sung throughout the country. Some of these are an unfortunate legacy from Victorian England. The music of these hymns is often indifferent, the words florid, sentimental and alien to the spirit of the people...."[1] The prevailing tendency in church music (as in all manner of things) is to import bodily from England or America. It may be noted that in the great majority of Irish dioceses the catechetical texts in use—with slight adaptations—are from the United States.

However, the opinion is growing, even if slowly, that in what concerns our liturgical and spiritual life we must seek our identity in what is our own. "Our vernacular music for the new liturgy should spring from our own culture, be composed by our own composers and have about it a native, an Irish quality."[2] In fact our religious songs in Irish are singularly beautiful as prayers and as music and suitable for use in public worship. In our new liturgical hymnals it is good to see a number of these songs. The increased popularity of our traditional music and ballads will lead, please God, to a knowledge and use of this traditional sacred music.

There is current in a number of dioceses what truly deserves the title "family liturgy". In fact it is the very liturgy itself, termed generally, the "Station Mass". A parish is divided up into "station" districts, and Mass is celebrated twice a year in different houses in each district (usually in spring and autumn), for which the neighbours gather in. Two priests attend and confessions are heard before Mass. The custom dates from Penal times when Mass was proscribed and had to be celebrated in secret. For various reasons the custom was kept up in many rural parts after the gaining of religious freedom. Even today the Station is, obviously, especially welcomed by the old and the infirm. In 1850, when the Irish hierarchy met in synod to shape the Irish Church of post-Penal days, one of the bishops summed up the pastoral, as distinct from the special sacramental, value of the Stations, when he spoke of the priests as "removing any scandals that exist, settling quarrels, cultivating friendship and charity with everybody and exercising the role of counsellors".[3]

[1] C. H. O'Callaghan, "Music in the New Liturgy", in *Irish Ecclesiastical Record*, cv:5 (1966), p. 286. The author was at the time Professor of Sacred Music in the National Seminary at Maynooth.
[2] *Ibid.*, p. 285.
[3] Cf. P. C. Barry, "The Legislation of the Synod of Thurles 1850", in *Irish Theological Quarterly* (April 1959).

The wonderful pastoral possibilities of this custom, in the light of what has happened and is happening since the Second Vatican Council, need no stressing, and we have some reports of what is being done.[4] Much depends on the zeal of the priest.

Another family practice of the highest importance is that of the family Rosary. We might term it the daily liturgy of the family. There is no doubt that the chief reason for the love and veneration in which the Rosary is held (even if some have been influenced by the current downgrading of the practice) is its connection with the Mass. In Penal times, above all, when so often it was impossible to get Mass, the Rosary was *the* prayer. Here is (in part) a translation of a typical offering of the Rosary:

> We offer up this Rosary in honour and in the name of Jesus and in honour of the glorious Virgin Mary, to share in the Holy Sacrifice of the Mass; with the same intention with which our Saviour offered himself on the tree of the Cross for our sake; with the intention of the Pope and the Roman Catholic Church; for every poor soul most severely suffering the pains of Purgatory, especially for our own poor dead if anything was lacking to them in confession or they were forgetful of Mass; may their pains be lessened, their glory increased; that the unbelievers of the world be converted to the right state and that those who are in the right state may remain in it. All this we ask of God and ask by virtue of these prayers. . . .

There are many variations of that offering, and some other prayers are usually added after the Rosary, for instance, the *Visita* of Compline. It has been well suggested that many of the petitions of those prayers that cluster round the family Rosary should be included in the Prayer of the Faithful in the Mass.[5] In fact we should be more aware of the great opportunity we now have, in accordance with the Constitution on the Liturgy (see especially par. 38), to integrate with the prayers of the Holy Sacrifice the

---

[4] Cf. *The Furrow*, XVII, 1 (1966), pp. 288, 381; XIX, 10 (1968), pp. 559–70.

[5] By Father Benedict, o.c.d., in an article on the prayers said before and after the family Rosary, *Knock Shrine Annual*, 1969, p. 33. In an interesting article in the *Ir. Eccl. Rec.*, CVI: 1 (1966), by John Hennig, on the Jewish "Berakah" and the Irish "Beannacht", we read (p. 10): "Nothing in present-day Christian life is closer to the home-liturgy preserved in Judaism than is the family Rosary. Equally close is the relationship between the candle lit by the pious Jew on the eve of Chanukkah and that placed in the windows of Irish homes on the eve of Christmas."

prayers and salutations of our people, which while being simple and direct, possess all the dignity of liturgical language. There are, thank God, stirrings in that direction, but there is need to make haste if the *Pobal Dé* (the People of God, as the Irish priest traditionally addresses his flock) of Ireland is to use its full potential at home and abroad in the life of the Church of God.

3. Herman Schmidt

A General View

THE STUDY of the liturgy has greatly improved the interpretation of ancient prayers although there is still much to be done. During this century there has been much discussion about the distinction between public and private prayer,[1] a subject that, freed from its former burden of extraneous juridical and canonical elements, can now proceed in its own right.

Now that the liturgy is celebrated in the vernacular and has taken on a more popular character, the non-liturgical prayers and songs deserve far more attention. During the last ten years, a vast literature has sprung up, not only about contemporary prayer in general with its peculiar problems,[2] but also about actual contemporary prayers. Since many of these texts are only destined for local practical use, they are difficult to get hold of.

To provide an international list of modern prayer-books is therefore a complicated business and this is borne out by the publishers who have helped with the collecting of these items. Any bibliography will be imperfect. The selection that follows is intended merely to exemplify certain critical points and to serve as a basis for further study.

A collection of records of contemporary religious music is indispensable. How can one judge religious songs without having

[1] The problem has been explained, with an extensive bibliography, in H. Schmidt, *Introductio in Liturgiam Occidentalem* (Rome, [3]1967), pp. 88–130: "Liturgia et Perfectio Christiana".
[2] Cf. the Editorial to this issue.

heard them?[3] One could go further and say that prayers and songs can only be judged properly when one prays or sings them oneself. When different texts and songs are regularly used for prayer before and after lectures or lessons, together with some factual information, the students will be able to judge these texts and melodies while praying or singing them.

If we follow this line, we shall probably agree on the following points: (a) to judge prayers and songs outside their proper context or situation, that is to say, from behind a desk or in some college, has little value and less authority; (b) to judge prayers and songs according to the language of academic theology, that is, without an ear for the language of prayer itself (the language of life, ordinary conversation, poetry or music) is fatal and irrelevant; (c) to subject modern prayers and songs exclusively to the cultural criteria of the old Latin repertoire, which is already more than one thousand years old, is to start with an irrelevant premise.

I. PRAYER BASED ON THE BIBLE

One cannot help but be struck by the biblical character of many prayers and songs today. These books try to make the word of Scripture relevant and so belong to the tradition of the Christian Churches.

(a) General Collections[4]

Some of the "revolutionary" collections carry an explanatory

[3] See H. Hucke, "Jazz and Folk Music in the Liturgy", in *Concilium* (Feb. 1969), pp. 69–85; U.S. volume 42.
[4] A. Auxilia (ed.), *Come è grande il tuo nome su tutta la terra*. Preghiere bibliche per ogni età e ogni vicenda della vita (Biblioteca dell gioventù, 11, Turin, 1967); C. Burke (ed.), *God is for Real, Man* (London and New York, [8]1967); F. Cebolla Lopez, *Plegarias del hombre nuevo* (Salamanca, 1963); *Prophetengebetbuch* (Munich, 1965); R. Raines, *Creative Brooding* (New York, [6]1968); A. Renard, *Prières de simplicité avec les évangiles des dimanches et fêtes* (Présence chrétienne, Paris, 1965); H. Schürmann, *Worte des Herrn* (Freiburg, 1968); Studies: J. de Fraine, *Prier avec la Bible; les antécédents bibliques des grandes prières chrétiennes* (Bruges, 1961). A. v. d. Drift, "Bidden uit de Bijbel", in *Eucharistia*, 60 (1968), 4, pp. 15–25; W. Fürst, *Der Geist des Gebets: Beten und Beter in der Bibel* (Stundenbuch 59, Hamburg, 1966); W. Neil, *The Plain Man looks at the Bible* (Fontana, London).

note. Thus Robert Raines provides "readings for thirty-four days to sharpen thought and provoke reflection. The daily format typically includes a reflection, two or three biblical passages, and a brief prayer or comment. Creative brooding produces action. So get ready every day to open a door (Rev. 3. 20), or pound on one (Luke 11. 5–20), to withhold a word (Matt. 7. 1), or speak one (Acts 9. 10–17; cf. 9. 17), to defer a visit (Rom. 15. 22) or make one (Acts 10; cf. 10. 23), to render an apology (Matt. 5. 23–4) or have a party (Luke 14. 1–24), to see a vision, dream a dream (Joel 2. 28; cf. Acts 2. 17). *Répondez, s'il vous plaît* (Answer, please)! Sing a song (Ps. 96. 1); jump over a wall! (Ps. 18. 29)."

Carl Burke has published "interpretations of Bible passages and stories, as told by some of God's bad-tempered angels with busted halos. This off-beat book is the result of an experiment in communication with adolescents in jail, camp and detention home settings."

Fermín Cebolla Lopez has edited a collection of prayers made by and with younger people: "Together we tried to make up prayers from the Bible itself. And so we built up, day by day, a collection of prayers that are wholly biblical, with only here and there a word or phrase to link one quotation with another. We tried all the time to let the gospel and St Paul speak for themselves."

(b) The "Our Father"

This occupies a key position in this development.[5] Many new translations have been attempted, with an eye on ecumenical agreement. Roger Hicks has provided a basis for group

[5] P. Bonnard, J. Dupont, F. Refoulé, *Notre Père qui es aux cieux: la prière oecuménique* (Cahiers de la Traduction Oecuménique de la Bible 3, Paris, 1968); R. Coste, *Notre Père sur le monde* (Spiritualité, Paris, 1966); W. Dirks, "Unser Vater; Rand- und Vorbemerkungen zu einem aktuellen Tatbestand", in *Hochland*, 60 (1968), pp. 193–200; G. Ebeling, *The Lord's Prayer in Today's World*, Living Church Books (London, 1966); R. Hicks, *The Lord's Prayer and Modern Man*: A Contemporary Approach (London, 1967); J. Pascher, "Das Vaterunser der Christen des deutschen Sprachgebietes", in *Liturgisches Jahrbuch*, 18 (1968), pp. 65–71; H. Thielicke, *The Prayer that Spans the World* (London, 1965).

discussion which raises questions prompted by the *Our Father* to which each member tries to give an answer.

(c) *The Psalms*

Although the Psalms are difficult, they remain a source of inspiration for a new kind of psalm.[6] Ernesto Cardenal, born 1925 in Nicaragua, was imprisoned and tortured in a concentration camp, became a monk, and now is involved in the development of the peasants. He has redressed David's psalms in modern clothes. The "I" of these psalms is both David and Cardenal, both Israel and the present community, and is always, first and last, the Messiah. The book is referred to as the "red catechism" of Latin American youth, and constitutes in part a theology of revolution.

In 1962 Raymond Hearn took a post as a teacher of religion in a London comprehensive school for boys. He managed to bring God close to this religiously heterogeneous group by means of the psalms. He edited a selection from some thousand psalms written by boys from twelve to sixteen.

Very different are the psalms composed by Ernst Eggiman, born in Berne in 1936. His mystical approach is strongly influenced by Zen Buddhism, but retains a Christian character. One senses the presence of Meister Eckhart in the background. His lyricism is influenced by the Japanese Haiku and Gomringer's concrete poetry. Less concise than these forms of lyricism, his own is more on the lines of a hymn and shows greater verbal richness, like American beat poetry.

Before passing on to other publications, I should point out that the more modern the prayers are, the more they show a biblical inspiration, even if one would not describe them as typical expressions of explicitly biblical piety.

---

[6] E. Cardenal, *Salmos* (Medellín, 1964; Avila, 1967); E. Eggiman, *Psalmen* (Limes Nova 18, Wiesbaden, 1967); R. Hearn, *Modern Psalms by Boys* (London, 1966); Studies: B. de Wit, "Kunnen wij de psalmen nog in gemeenschap bidden?", in *Tijdschrift voor Liturgie*, 52 (1968), pp. 105–19; P. Drijvers, "Psalmen bidden", in *Eucharistia*, 60 (1968), 4, pp. 26–35; P. Emery, *La méditation de l'Ecriture et des psaumes* (Taizé, ⁴1967); A. Rose, *Psaumes et prière chrétienne* (Coll. de Pastorale Liturgique, 66, Saint-André, 1965).

II. Collections and Anthologies

In recent years there has been an increase in this field. The prayers are gathered from all ages and religions. They are basically traditional. The editors are not concerned with time, place or religion, but include what they think valuable as an expression of prayer for all times and all places, so that it can serve at least as an inspiration.

(a) *General Collections*[7]

Apart from the Latin liturgical heritage, these collections are indispensable for the liturgy as it is now developing, since this liturgy must now be open to all the genuine prayers and religious songs of all cultures.

Among the classics, I would mention the collections of Alfonso Di Nola, Christoph Einiger, H. Finberg, E. Goudge and W. and F. von Hahn with Walter Nigg. *Courtes prières*, Manfred Seitz and Friedrich Thiele, Fulton Sheen and John Wallace Suter are

---

[7] F. Cebolla Lopez and J. Sierra Benayas (eds.), *Plegarias de todos los hombres* (Estela 67, Salamanca, ²1968); R. Claude and J. Feder (eds.), *Prie dans le secret: recueil de prières* (Tournai, 1966); F. Colquhoun (ed.), *Parish Prayers* (London, 1967); *Courtes prières pour le chrétien dans le siècle: textes choisis et présentés par les Moines de la Pierre-qui-vire* (Bruges, 1965). A. Di Nola (ed.), *La preghiera dell' uomo: antologia delle preghiere di tutti i tempi e di tutti i popoli* (Parma, 1957); C. Einiger (ed.), *Die schönsten Gebete der Welt*; der Glaube grosser Persönlichkeiten (Munich, ³1967); H. Finberg (ed.), *Manual of Catholic Prayer* (London, 1962); *Gott ist gegenwärtig: Gebete evangelischer Frömmigkeit* (Munich, 1968); E. Goudge (ed.), *A Diary of Prayer* (London, 1966); *Groot Gebedenboek* (Utrecht); W. and F. von Hahn (ed.), *Brevier des Alltags: Meditationem und Gebete aus 20 christlichen Jahrhunderten* (Pfaffenhofen-Ulm, 1966); W. Nigg (ed.), *Gebete der Christenheit* (Munich, ²1967); W. Nigg (ed.), *Gott ist gegenwärtig: Gebete evangelischer Frömmigkeit* (Munich, 1967); *Prayers New and Old* (London, 1966); *Prière simple: petit recueil de prières* (Taizé, 1966); *Recueil de formules de prière universelle* (Paris, 1967); N. de Robeck (ed.), *Praise the Lord, an anthology* (Chicago, 1967); M. Seitz and F. Thiele (eds.), *Wir beten: Gebete für Menschen von heute* (Bad Salzuflen, ²1968); Fulton Sheen (ed.), *That Tremendous Love*, an anthology of inspirational quotations, poems, prayers and philosophical comments (New York, 1967); P. Strodach (ed.), *Oremus*, collects, devotions, litanies from ancient and modern sources (Minneapolis, 1966); J. Suter (ed.), *Prayers for a New World* (New York, 1964).

definitely intended for man today. Two "Eastern" collections have recently been published by the Russian Orthodox Church.[8]

(b) *Personalities*[9]

We need more collections of prayers from the Fathers of the Church and the ancient spiritual writers. Collections from the past retain their value. People also like the prayers of well-known modern personalities. A theologian should be particularly interested in such prayers as those of Søren Kierkegaard. One should also have a look at the prayers of Peter Marshall, who, as Chaplain of the United States' Senate, led prayers for many years when Congress was sitting.

III. NEW PRAYERS

It is really impossible to discern dominating trends in the multitude of modern prayer-books.[10] Since we can only mention

[8] *The Art of Prayer*: an Orthodox anthology, trans. from the Russian (London, 1966); K. Rose (ed.), *Christ ist erstanden; Osterglaube in der russischen Dichtung* (Berlin, 1966).

[9] Anselmus Cantuariensis, *Gebete*, trans. by L. Helbling (Sigillum 24, Einsiedeln, 1965); Augustinus Hipponensis, *Lobpreis und Anbetung*, trans. by J. Mader (Vienna, 1966); S. Kierkegaard, *The Prayers*, ed. with a new interpretation of his life and thought, by P. Lefevre (Chicago, [3]1965); P. Marshall, *The Prayers*, ed. with prefaces by C. Marshall (New York, [18]1954); E. Reynolds (ed.), *The Heart of Thomas More*; readings for every day of the year, selection (London, 1966); E. Przywara, *The Heart of John Newman*, a synthesis, with an introduction by H. Davis (London, 1963).

[10] G. Appleton, *One Man's Prayers* (London, 1967); J. Baillie, *A Diary of Private Prayer* (London, 1936); W. Barclay, some fifteen prayer-books have been published by SCM and Collins (London); C. Benito Plaza, *Oraciones para cuando llegue la noche* (Bilbao, 1967); A. Bittleston, *Meditative Prayers for Today* (London, [7]1966); M. Boyd, *Are You Running with Me, Jesus?* (London, 1967); M. Boyd, *Book of Days* (London, 1968); R. Castle, "Litany of the Ghetto", in *New Christian* (2 June 1966); R. Castle, *Prayers from a Burned-Out City*; Abbey of Maria Frieden (ed.), *Christus-Gebete* (Munich, 1968); Sister Corita (Mary Corita Kent), *Footnotes and Headlines*: A Play-Pray Book (New York, 1967); G. Courtois, *You Who Are Sent*, prayers for the apostolate (New York, 1966); W. Gössmann, *Wörter suchen Gott*, Gebetstexte, mit einem religionspädagogischen Nachwort von G. Stachel (Unterweisen und Verkünden 5, Einsiedeln, 1968); C. Herzel, *Prayers of the People of God* (Philadelphia, 1967); D. Hurley, *Everyday Prayer Book* (London, 1966); L. Jerphagnon, *Nostre*

a limited number, we shall have to limit ourselves to a few observations.

Most of what is published continues the tradition without any major upheavals, and this holds particularly for the many works of William Barclay. Some authors are a little more revolutionary and therefore frequently discussed. Among these Malcolm Boyd, with whom C. S. Lewis used to correspond, is well known.[11] Here I quote a prayer whose ending is also the title of the book: "It's morning, Jesus. It's morning, and here's that light and sound all over again. I've got to move fast... get into the bathroom, wash up, grab a bite to eat, and run some more. I just don't feel like it, Lord. What I really want to do is get back into bed, pull up the covers, and sleep. All I seem to want today is the big sleep, and here I've got to run all over again. Where am I running? You know these things I can't understand. It's not that I need to have you tell me. What counts most is just that somebody knows, and it's you. That helps a lot. So I'll follow along, okay? But lead, Lord. Now I've got to run. Are you running with me, Jesus?" In his *Book of Days* (thoughts for every day of the year) the 11 October entry is: "Are you bombing with me, Jesus?"—the text of a poster carried in a peace demonstration in San Francisco in the spring of 1967.

More interesting still is Sister Corita's Play-Pray Book of which the blurb says: "*Footnotes and Headlines* is for that whole new generation of people in every way of life, of every faith and of no known faith (and of every age), who are turned off by the very idea of a 'Prayer-book'. This is a serious book for people

preghiere (Vicenza); J. Jones, *Prayers for the People,* a memorial collection of pulpit prayers (Richmond, 1968); Kelley, *Men before God,* prayers and thoughts (Westminster, 1962); W. Lindenberg, *Die Menschheit betet,* Praktiken der Meditation in der Welt (Munich); A. Maltha, *Nieuwe gebeden* (Nijmegen, 1965); E. Martin, *Talking to God* (London); A. Müller-Felsenburg, *Gott und Co.: Gebeten eines renitenten Laien* (Friedberg); W. Opel, "Seeing and Praying", in *New Christian* (8 Sept. 1966); W. Purcell, *The Plain Man Looks at Himself* (London); D. Sölle and F. Steffensky (eds.), *Das politische Nachtgebet in Köln* (Mainz, 1969); A. Stöger, *In Christus Jesus: Gebete des Neuen Bundes* (Vienna, 1964); J. Vandenberg, *Leven zonder grenzen: overwegingen; verzinnebeeld in zeskleurige tekeningen* (Bruges, 1967); L. Weatherhead, *A Private House of Prayer* (London, ⁶1966).
[11] Cf. M. Boyd, *Are You Running...?,* Introduction.

who refuse to take themselves seriously." The important book by Wilhelm Gössmann, well known for his study of sacred language, is of a different kind.[12] Alfred Müller-Felsenburg gave his prayers the title: "Prayers of a rebellious layman" (*Gebeten eines reniten-ten Laien*). The political night-prayers of Cologne, edited by Dorothee Sölle and Fulbert Steffensky, are a contemporary phenomenon and so a sign of contradiction.

Because the prayer-books of Louis Evely, Romano Guardini, Jacques Lebret, P. Lyonnet, Michel Quoist and Karl Rahner are already widely known they have not been listed in the bibliography.

(a) *Africa*[13]

Fritz Pawelzik, a youth leader who worked for the CJMV in Ghana, gathered examples of the way in which some fifteen Christians talked to the Father in an anthology. These prayers are exceptional for their simplicity, their concrete approach and their imagery.

(b) *Negro Spirituals and Beatles*[14]

These two genres do not belong together but are mentioned together here for practical reasons in order to draw attention to only a few publications selected from a large quantity. The collections mentioned in the bibliography are a useful introduction to the spirituals. As to the Beatles, it is worth looking through all their lyrics. In a study of them by Georg Geppert, Karl Rahner says in his Foreword: "A preacher of the Word of God should be in touch with the Beatles' fans if he is to avoid preaching only his own predilections. These songs provide a sound

[12] W. Gössmann, *Sakrale Sprache* (Theologische Fragen Heute 3, Munich, 1965).

[13] F. Pawelzik (ed.), *Ich liege auf meiner Matte und bete* (Wuppertal) and *Ich singe dein Lob durch den Tag* (Wuppertal, 1965); there is an English edn. of the first, entitled *I Lie on My Mat and Pray*; J. Nketia, *Prayers at Kple Worship* (Africa, 1963); B. Nyom, *Prière biblique et prière négro-africaine* (1965); O. Wermter, "Gotteserlebnis im Negerkral", in *Orientierung*, 32 (1968), 9, pp. 110–11.

[14] The Beatles, *Complete Works* (Amsterdam, 1969); G. Geppert (ed.), *Songs der Beatles* (Munich, 1968); K. Hansen (ed.), *Go down, Moses*; 100 Spirituals and Gospel Songs; M. Stewart (ed.), *Gospel Song Book* (London, 1968).

introduction to the Beatle fans who find in them their own experience of life."

IV. Prayer from Birth to Death

Now that the liturgy has rediscovered the people, its prayer must obviously integrate the ordinary life of these people. Paraliturgical prayer has always taken this point very seriously, whatever we may think of its quality.

(a) Family and Youth [15]

These are extremely important for the growth of the new liturgy if we do not want the life of the family to be reduced to a purely biological factor which, according to some, has no longer any social part to play in a secularized world. Very little material is available.

There are many prayer-books for the sick and the dying. There is also an immense literature connected with devotions, various schools of spirituality, and the veneration of the saints. Although this is no doubt an important sector, there is no room to deal with it here. We therefore only mention prayers used for grace before and after meals[16] the examination of conscience,[17] and prayers for unity among Christians.[18]

---

[15] A.C., "Liturgie als Formprinzip in der katholischen Familie", in *Liturgie und Mönchtum*, 19 (1956), pp. 62-6; F. Barbero (ed.), *Osiamo dire* (Turin, 1968); Th. Bogler (ed.), "Die Familie, Gotteswerk und Menschenmühen", in *Liturgie und Mönchtum*, 23 (1958); H. Caffarel, *Présence à Dieu: cent lettres sur la prière*, spec. nr. of L'Anneau d'or (Paris, 1967); J. Cassidy and B. Sharratt, *Come to the Lord: An Assembly Book for Secondary Schools* (London, 1968); *Dein Reich komme: Gebete für junge Christen* (Würzburg, 1957); Mother St Dominic, *Prayers for Young Christians: An Assembly Book for Secondary Schools* (London, 1966); T. Goffi, *Spiritualità familiare* (Famiglia e Pastorale, Rome, ³1968); C. Janssens, D. Mous and N. Nooren, *Thuis bidden* ('s-Hertogenbosch, 1967); Kelly, *Youth before God: Prayers and Thoughts* (Westminster, 1957); M. Kitson, *Infant Prayer* (London, ³1967); F. Lelotte, *Giovani verso Cristo* (Rome); W. Wilson, *Hymns for Young Christians* (London, 1967).

[16] M. Bouyer, *Table Prayer* (New York, 1967); J. Hennig, "Zur Stellung des Tischgebets in der Liturgie", in *Liturgisches Jahrbuch*, 18 (1968), pp. 87-98.

[17] L. Rosadoni, *Cuore d'uomo—cuore di Dio* (Turin, 1968).

[18] P. Rouillard (ed.), *Le Livre de l'unité* (Paris, 1966); *New Hymns for*

V. The Liturgy

(a) *Studies*

A few studies of a general nature are important for our subject.[19] Walter Dürig's study of the concept of *"pietas"* is a classic. Albert Höfer, Ernst Lange and Gerhard Schnath deal with contemporary liturgical problems. These problems are also constantly discussed in the periodicals.[20]

(b) *The Eucharist*

Although the Latin Mass is now celebrated in the vernacular, the need for free texts is still acute. A few publications have sharpened the issue.[21]

---

a New Day, publ. by the World Council of Churches; P. Scheele, *Vater, die Stunde ist da: Gebete der Oekumene* (Freiburg, 1964).

[19] W. Dürig, *Pietas Liturgica: Studien zum Frommigkeitsbegriff und zur Gottesvorstellung der abendländischen Liturgie* (Regensburg, 1958); A. Höfer, *Modelle einer pastoralen Liturgie: Vorschlage zur Reform* (Offene Fragen, Graz, 1969); E. Lange, *Chancen des Alltags: Ueberlegungen zur Funktion des christlichen Gottesdienstes in der Gegenwart* (Stuttgart, ²1966); G. Schnath (ed.), *Fantasie für Gott: Gottesdienste in neuer Gestalt*, commissioned by the Deutsche Evangelische Kirchentag (Stuttgart, ²1965).

[20] J. Beex, "Gebed—stilte—rust", in *Tijdschr. voor Liturgie*, 49 (1965), pp. 319-23; Th. Bogler (ed.), "Frömmigkeit", in *Liturgie und Mönchtum*, 27 (1960); M. Collins, "Presidential Prayer in the Liturgy", in *Proclamation and Confession of the Christian Mystery* (1967); D. Cremer, "Das Wort als Begegnung und Fülile: zum Beten des Christen in der Kirche Christi", in *Liturgie und Mönchtum*, 29 (1961), pp. 37-50; J. Grootaers, "De spanningen tussen liturgisch en persoonlijk gebed in het verleden", in *Tijdschrift voor Liturgie*, 46 (1962), pp. 5-9; L. van Holk, "Robinson over liturgie en gebed", in *Wending*, 18 (1963), pp. 771-82; J. Hupperetz and M. Stijfs, "Liturgie et gebed", in *Tijdschr. voor Liturgie*, 46 (1962), pp. 385-8; L. Leloir, *Liturgie et prière personelle* (1965); L. Leloir, "Vers une liturgie plus priante", in *Nouv. Rev. Théol.*, 85 (1963), pp. 1023-38; T. Maeder, "Towards a theology of prayer", in *Worship*, 40 (1966), pp. 218-30; Th. Maertens, "Prière et rencontre", in *Paroisse et Liturgie*, 48 (1966), pp. 3-18; K. Müller, "Das Gebet im Leben der Gemeinde", in *Jahrbuch für Liturgik und Hymnologie*, 9 (1964), pp. 1-28; A. Schoenen, "Das immerwährende Gebet", in *Liturgie und Möchtum*, 27 (1960), pp. 72-86; E. von Severus, "Liturgie und persönliche Frömmigkeit", in *Liturgie und Mönchtum*, 9 (1951), pp. 9-16; W. Simpson, *Jewish Prayer and Worship* (London, 1965); H. Wegman, "'Wat is dan de mens, dat gij aan hem denkt?' Het gebed in de liturgie", in *Theologie en Pastoraat*, 64 (1968), pp. 96-111.

[21] R. Berthier, *Vivante parole: pour vivre la Messe* (Limoges, 1967); P.

(c) *The Choral Office, the Breviary and the Readings*

The undercurrent of unrest here was brought to the fore at the congress organized by the group that bears the name "Liturgie et Monastères" in the "Fraternité des Dominicaines de Méry-sur-Oise", 1–4 July 1968.[22]

The trouble with the breviary is so well known that there is no need to discuss it here. There is general agreement that the priests should be offered as soon as possible a kind of daily prayer which fits in with their daily tasks, whether liturgical or not.

A new kind of spiritual reading for each day of the year has appeared (many in Italy). These collections are traditional in that they incorporate texts from all ages. They are distinguished by the introduction of readings from world-literature, seen as part of the tradition and in a certain sense a continuation of the "spiritual books" strictly so called.[23]

(d) *The Netherlands and Flanders*

Liturgy in the Netherlands and Flanders has undergone some exciting developments. This is also the case elsewhere, especially in the United States. But because Holland's efforts have been sensationally reported in the world press, widespread interest has been aroused.

In Holland there are centres which distribute texts. The most

---

Bruylants, "Op zoek naar een nieuwe stijl in de vertaling van de gebeden van het missaal", in *Tijdschrift voor Liturgie*, 48 (1964), pp. 295–9; Bulst, *Wir beten an: eucharistische Gebete für das Kirchenjahr* (Kevelaer, ³²1966); G. Danneels and Th. Maertens, *La prière eucharistique: formes anciennes et conception nouvelle du canon de la messe* (Vivante Liturgie 79, Paris, 1967); A. Schilling, *Orationen der Messe in Auswahl: ein Beitrag zum Problem ihrer Uebertragung in unsere Zeit* (Essen, ⁴1968).

[22] "L'office divin aujourd'hui", in *La Maison-Dieu*, 95 (1968), pp. 1–141; see also A. de Vogué, "Kultus of kontemplatie? De bedoeling van het getijdengebed bij Benedictus", in *Tijdschr. voor Liturgie*, 51 (1967), pp. 424–47; A. de Vogué, "Le sens de l'office divine d'après la Règle de S. Benoît", in *Rev. d'Asc. et de Myst.*, 168 (1966), pp. 389–404 and 169 (1967), pp. 21–33.

[23] O. Dudzus (ed.), *Bonhoeffer Brevier* (Munich, 1963); B. Manfredi (ed.), *"Prima che il gallo canti mi rinnegherai tre volte"* (Fossano, 1968); A. Pronzato (ed.), *Il Guastafeste: breviario di rimorsi* (Turin, 1967); L. Rusca, (ed.), *Il breviario dei laici* (Milan, ⁶1965); M. Tosco (ed.), *Alzo zero: provocazione quotidiane per vincere l'isolamento in questo mondo tutto da rifare* (Turin, 1968).

important centre in Holland is the liturgical publisher, N. V. Gooi en Sticht, Hilversum. It covers the whole Dutch Province and uses advanced methods of publication and organization. It also produces a series of records for practical instruction under the name of "Didascalia". It publishes the whole eucharistic service for every Sunday and every feast separately in both large and small format for the priests and the faithful, and the whole is given the title of "Source of Christian Spirit" (*Bron van christelijke geest*).

No book has been published in Holland which gives us a synthesis of all that is going on; it is considered to be superfluous since everybody knows these celebrations of the liturgy from experience. A detailed study of the liturgy in Holland has, however, appeared in Germany.[24]

Some modest publications may be grouped together as texts for the ordinary liturgical services[25] and books of song.[26] The workgroup for the liturgy in the vernacular (*Werkgroep voor Volkstaal-liturgie*) is well known and consists of a team of liturgists, biblical scholars, writers and musicians. The poet, Huub Oosterhuis, has had some of his work translated.[27] Huub Oosterhuis and Michel van der Plas, together with the biblical scholars Pius

[24] A. Schilling, *Fürbitten und Kanongebete der höllandischen Kirche: Materialien zur Diskussion um zeitgemässe liturgische Texte* (Essen, [5]1968).

[25] W. Barnard, *Gebeden in de gemeente: teksten, folder 1: Advent, Kerstmis, Uitvaart* (Antwerp, 1968); W. Barnard, *Gebeden voor de gemeente die zich op het Pascha voorbereid: teksten* (Antwerp, 1969); R. van den Bosch, *Alle eer en glorie* (Helmond, [5]1967); R. van den Bosch, *Wij vieren feest* (Helmond, [2]1957); R. van den Bosch, *Schriftlezingen en gebeden voor vigile en ochtend van de uitvaart der overleden gelovigen* (Haarlem, 1966); K. Douven and Th. van Houtert, *Levende liturgie* (Nijmegen, 1967); *Liturgisch kerkboek* (Malines, 1965); W. Reckman, Ph. Stein and W. ter Burg (eds.), *Werkmap voor liturgie* (Hilversum); Ph. Stein, *De dienst van de maaltiid* (Voorburg, 1966); *Zolang er mensen zijn* (Hilversum, [2]1967).

[26] I. De Sutter, *Een kerk die zingt* (Antwerp, 1962); I. De Sutter, *Een nieuw lied* (Antwerp, [3]1962); G. Helderenberg, *Nieuwe kerkliederen* (Antwerp, 1965); Th. Naastepad, *Op de dorsvloer* (Hilversum, 1964); "Het nieuwe kerklied", in *Ontmoeting*, 15 (1962), numbers 7 and 8.

[27] H. Oosterhius, *Your Word is Near* (New York, 1968); H. Oosterhuis, *Hand op mijn hoofd* (Utrecht, 1965); H. Oosterhuis, *In het voorbijgaan* (Utrecht, 1968).

Drijvers and Han Renckens, have published a new translation of fifty psalms which is noteworthy.[28]

Sometimes special occasions prompted special texts, as happened for the funeral of Bishop Willem Bekkers, of 's-Hertogenbosch.[29]

A modest beginning has been made with the publication of readings for every day of the year, taken from old and new sources.[30]

[28] H. Oosterhuis, M. van der Plas, with the co-operation of P. Drijvers and H. Renckens, *Fifty Psalms* (London and New York, 1969).

[29] "Eucharistieviering met toeristen", in *Theologie en Pastoraat*, 63 (1967), pp. 113–28 and 64 (1968), pp. 113–28; Funeral of Mgr Bekkers: *Bisschop Bekkers* (Utrecht, 1966), pp. 421–44.

[30] J. Kocken and M. Sterke (ed.), *In dienst van het Woord*, commissioned by the Intermonasteriële Werkgroep voor Liturgie and the Sectie Liturgie voor Religieuzen, in consultation with the Dutch Commission for the Liturgy (Haarlem, 1968 f.).

Translated by Theo Westow

PART III
DOCUMENTATION
CONCILIUM

Placid Murray

The Language of
Christian Worship

FOUR major problems are felt today in the language of Christian worship: the impact of the mass media, the use of biblical imagery in modern speech, the need for a spoken style in liturgical texts, and finally, the very nature of language itself and its function. These four areas were dealt with in detail at the first general meeting of Societas Liturgica, the international society for liturgical research and renewal, which was held at Glenstal Abbey, Ireland, 2–5 September 1969.

The findings of the conference may be outlined as follows. The language of the mass media is not poetical but coldly descriptive, and the wide dissemination of the media has brought about a diminution of vocabulary all along the line, but especially in the theological world. Long before the advent of the mass media, the whole section of the historic Christian vocabulary was becoming arcane to a large number of lay people. The only effect of the media was to hasten its eclipse. While we may lament these ravages of contemporary culture on common speech, we have no option but to adjust the language of worship accordingly, since common speech is the stuff with which we have to work. In all probability the liturgies of tomorrow will contain less language; most of our historic liturgies are overloaded with words, dating from a time when the verbal was the only means of communication. The new "non-linear", co-expressive language in which image and word are forged into a synthesis is already being used in many places in worship, particularly in the United States. In the discussions which followed Professor Skoglund's and Dr

Hageman's papers, there was general agreement that a new dimension of communication in worship was being opened up here, but that once we have recovered from the first shock of the new media we shall still find ourselves faced with the necessity for language in liturgy.

With regard to the use of biblical imagery in a vernacular liturgy, the current problems of the various language areas, though not identical, are nevertheless remarkably similar. Thus, for instance, versions of the Bible produced in Spain are uncongenial to the idioms of Latin America. As regards English, no one existing version was felt to meet the needs of the liturgy in the required combination of clarity, contemporary usage, and quality of style. What is needed is a total re-structuring of a kind native to the modern language in question, whether Spanish, English or any other language. The expertise needed here is not that of the exegete, nor of the liturgist, but of the master of literary style. A workshop had been conducted at the conference in which the biblical readings for Easter Sunday were translated directly from the Greek with a view to liturgical use. This group, under the leadership of Dr Russell of Belfast, reported that before translation is undertaken it would be necessary to select the readings. Thus the first step would be an agreed lectionary. This would enable translators to treat each Lesson as a unit and give it a beginning that would make more sense of the meaning. Punctuation is also an important factor in a liturgical Bible, for the person who is to read aloud to a congregation needs more guidance as to where he should pause, so that the people who are listening can understand.

The third major issue debated at the conference was the provision of a spoken style in the liturgical texts. Two factors are involved in up-dating archaic language; they are vocabulary and syntax. The more conservative may see the need to remove archaic words and substitute ones that are understood today. But to stop here is only to tinker with the problem. The problem of syntax (that is the grammatical construction of the sentences) is a much bigger and more difficult one. At the time of the Reformation, liturgical texts were taken from Latin originals, but in the process of translation the Latin syntax and rhetorical forms were retained. This was perhaps admissible at a time when many people were familiar with Latin. But European languages have changed much over the past four hundred years, and the process of change is accelerating. The old-fashioned main clause with dependent clauses making up a long and complicated sentence-structure has disappeared. Sentences are now shorter and more staccato. Fewer adjectives are used, and the style tends to be terse and bald.

In the provision of modern liturgical texts, it is necessary to remember that they will either be spoken aloud or sung. In either case a certain rhythm is required, and a careful consideration of the juxtaposition of consonant sounds so that the reader may be able to enunciate clearly and convey the meaning without undue difficulty. So far as texts for singing are concerned it is important that musicians be involved at all stages so that their specialist knowledge may facilitate the eventual creation of something which is in fact singable. When acceptable music eventually emerges, the sung text will tend to be more lasting than texts which are merely said, for the association of music and words makes a more lasting impression on the person than words alone can do.

With regard to the function of language in worship, the conference devoted its first day to Professor H. Schmidt's paper on the subject.

Each area of human life has its own particular way of using language and uses its own particular technical terminology. It is therefore impossible to avoid using "religious" terms in liturgy. But these should be kept to the minimum, bearing in mind that the worshipping community is made up of people from many walks of life, and will also contain people who have a minimal knowledge of the Christian faith. However, it is not necessary that people in a liturgical service should understand every word; but they should have a clear impression of the significance of the act of worship. The language of the liturgy should be such as to have the maximum impact for the maximum number of people present. Because the liturgy is an *activity* it is not in practice profitable to discuss liturgical language in isolation from liturgical action. The distinction between "language" and *"langue"* is most valuable and important in this connection.

Such a liturgy will not be developed at the desks of scholars, but will spring from the life of the Church. No doubt scholars have their part to play, but the evolution of this pattern of worship will involve members of the Church at every level. To speak of liturgy as evolving is not to assume that the liturgies of the past were wrong and must now be corrected. Indeed, the creation of a liturgical form suitable to the needs of our age carries with it the implication that in this world of change the liturgy must continually be renewed so that it can be relevant to the human situation and to men's understanding of the reality of God.

Societas Liturgica has chosen as its theme for its next conference "The Theological Background to Experimental Liturgies". This further conference will be organized by the incoming chairman, Canon R. C. D. Jasper, D.D., 1 Little Cloister, Westminster Abbey, London, S.W.1.

Erhard Quack

Contemporary Church Music

DURING a study week in Turin (1–6 September 1969) arranged by the international student group Universa Laus, new liturgical music from around twenty countries was staged and discussed (about sixty pieces in all). As Father Gelineau said when the conference opened, the object was not to stage a systematic survey, but to provide some more general information about what was being done in the field of liturgical music, whether this showed a high standard of composition or, as was sometimes the case, whether it was still at a relatively primitive stage. Individual pieces of music were presented and the subsequent discussion by experts maximized the exchange of experience and stimulated interest in the production of new texts and new music.

The new role of church music and its composer was the subject of the main paper (Heinrich Rennings). As singing and music are integral parts of the liturgy, the composer's function is to collaborate in the creation of liturgy. Because it is an integral part of the liturgy, music cannot escape the process of liturgical renewal. The justification and value of this renewal must be demonstrable in terms of the contemporary situation in which the liturgical forms and signs—music and singing among them—are required to express our faith and our consciousness of God's presence among us.

The pieces selected were presented in fourteen sessions. Groups were formed for the study of specific items: entrance songs, preaching; psalms; hymns (songs); prayers. A further group devoted itself to a detailed examination and discussion of music in contemporary rhythm. During these sessions the complete score was projected on to a screen while the music was being played. The group leader briefly described the origin, structure and purpose of each piece. Subsequent discussion was undertaken by the experts present and centred on the manner in which contemporary church music has to take into account new ideas about the significance of liturgical structures, the role of singing, and the use of musical instruments. Other people present were expected to join in the discussions. The conference administration was efficient and members of the student group overcame language difficulties by supplying simultaneous translations.

The music ranged from folk to classical, from congregational singing to *virtuoso* choir and solo pieces, from improvised guitar accompaniment to full orchestra. Appropriately enough, given the changed liturgical situation and the structure of the contemporary community, simple musical arrangements predominated. Among the many composers whose work was played were Huijbers, Misch, Blarr, Krenek, de Fatto, Woll, Senator, Manzano, Prophette, Eben, Schieri, Zimmermann, Trexler, Arguello, Connolly, Berthier, Giombini, Kendall, Puig, Meister, Paccagnini and Williams.

In a final session, the writer summarized the conference's conclusions, and observed that contemporary liturgical music displayed two characteristic features: first, variety of musical style has replaced the relative uniformity sacred music once had; secondly, it was noticeable that the old uniformity had lost its hold on account of the new flexibility of liturgical structures, a flexibility that had less to do with predetermined rubrics than with local liturgical requirements together with the religious and sociological structure of the celebrating community.

I also mentioned the emergence of five particular points during the discussions that followed the performance of the various pieces of music. First, the dominant interest in folk music as a consequence of active participation by the congregation. Among the peoples of Southern Europe this could be seen in the use they made of popular profane music, whereas the tendency among their northern neighbours was to adapt and make greater use of existing church songs.

Secondly, an increase in the popularity of part-singing. Spontaneous and improvised singing was an aspect of this. Thirdly, an enthusiasm for rhythm, the trend that more than any other runs counter to the traditional forms of church music.

Fourthly—and closely connected with my third point—more use of musical instruments and a wider range to choose from. Indeed, any instrument is admissible. Finally, and in contrast to the more basic trends mentioned so far, there is a tendency to demand higher musical standards though without any wish to lose contact with popular musical idioms. There were several pieces that successfully resolved the tensions that can emerge in this connection (Eben; Krenek).

By the end of the conference it was clear to all participants that, though to a large extent still at the experimental stage, much had been and was being done to ensure that Vatican II's liturgical *aggiornamento* was reflected in church music. There is an obvious drive to break free from rubrical bondage and clear the way for a more natural and informal expression of worship in music and song.

Concluding the conference, Father Gelineau outlined some areas of future development. Referring to the opening paper, he reminded us that fundamentally liturgy is a matter of communication between God and man and that the manifestation of this connection requires signs that we can make sense of. Church music that hopes to remain permanently an acceptable form of expression cannot afford to ignore this.

The conference, which ended with a multi-language Eucharist, was considered a notable success.

Translated by Simon King

Biographical Notes

DOMENICO BILOTTI, s.j., born 26 November 1934 in Italy, ordained 1962. He studied at Milan and Naples, and at the Pontificio Istituto Liturgico (Rome). He holds a licentiate in theology and philosophy and is now working for his doctorate in theology of the liturgy. He lectures in liturgy in Naples and Rome and is the author of *Preghiere Liturgiche* (1968).

GERARD BROCCOLO, born 14 June 1939 in Chicago, ordained 1964. He studied at the Gregorian and at the Pontificio Istituto Liturgico (Rome), gaining his licentiate in theology and master's degree in liturgy. He is now Professor of Liturgy at St Mary of the Lake seminary, Mundelein (U.S.A.), and Secretary to the Commission for the Sacred Liturgy of the Chicago Archdiocese.

JAN VAN CAUWELAERT, born 12 April 1914 in Belgium, ordained 1939, consecrated bishop 1954. He studied at the University of Louvain and gained his licentiate in philosophy. He was Bishop of Inongo (Congo) from 1959 to 1967. He is the author of various articles on missionary aspects of liturgy and ecumenism.

JOSEPH GELINEAU, s.j., born 31 October 1920 in France, ordained in 1951. He studied at the Institut Catholique (Paris) and at the Pontificio Istituto Orientale (Rome). He gained a doctorate in theology in 1960, and is now professor of pastoral liturgy at the Institut Supérieur de Pastorale Catéchétique in Paris. He is a member of the French National Centre for Pastoral Liturgy, editor of the review *Eglise qui chante*, and a member of the governing body of "Universa Laus". He has composed much liturgical music and is the author of numerous articles on liturgy and of *Voices and Instruments in Christian Worship* (1965).

MARK GIBBARD, born 6 April 1910 in England, was ordained in the Anglican Church in 1933. He studied at Cambridge University and at Cuddesdon Theological College (Oxford), gaining his M.A. in theology. He is a member of the Society of St John the Evangelist. His publications include *Unity is not Enough* (1965), and *Should We Pray?* (1969).

ARCHBISHOP DENIS HURLEY, O.M.I., was born on 9 November 1915 in Cape Town, ordained in 1939, consecrated bishop in 1951. He studied in Rome at the Angelicum and at the Gregorian, gaining licentiate's degrees in theology and philosophy. He has been Archbishop of Durban since 1951. He is the author of various articles on questions of race, human dignity, freedom in the Church, and so on.

ROBERT LEDOGAR, C.F.M.S., born 3 August 1933 in New York, ordained in 1959. He studied at the Maryknoll Seminary and at Fordham University, and in Paris at the Institut Catholique, doctoring in theology in 1964. He now teaches at Maryknoll. His publications include *Acknowledgment: Praise-Verbs in the Early Greek Anaphora* (1968).

PLACID MURRAY, O.S.B., born 7 October 1918 in Ireland, ordained 1941. He studied at Maredsous and at the Anselmo, Rome, doctoring in theology in 1964. He is a monk of Glenstal Abbey. He is a consultor to the Irish National Liturgical Commission and I.C.E.L. He is the author of *The Canon of the Mass* (1961).

DIARMUID O'LAOGHAIRE, S.J., born 1 August 1915 in Dublin, ordained 1948. Studied at University College, Dublin, and at the University of Wales, gaining his M.A. and doctorate in Celtic Philology. He now teaches in a Dublin secondary school. His publications include *Irish Spirituality* (1957); *Our Mass Our Life: Some Irish Traditions and Prayers* (1968).

JAN PETERS, O.C.D., born 25 April 1921 in The Netherlands, ordained in 1946. He studied at the universities of Louvain and Nijmegen, doctoring in theology in 1957. From 1949–66 he taught dogmatic theology at his Order's House of Studies (Smakt-Venray) in The Netherlands. Since 1966 he has been Assistant Secretary to the *Concilium* General Secretariat, and a consultant to the Dutch Pastoral Council since 1967. His publications include *Geloof en mystiek. Een theologische bezinning op de geestelijke werken van de St Jan van het Kruis* (1957); *Volledige werken van de H. Johannes van het Kruis* (1963); and *God tegemoet* (²1963).

DAVID POWER, O.M.I., born 14 December 1932 in Dublin, ordained 1964. Studied at the Pontificio Istituto Liturgico (Rome) and doctored in theology (1968). He is now superior at his Order's House of Studies, Piltown, Ireland, where he teaches liturgy.

IANTHE PRATT was born on 7 December 1926 in London and is a Catholic. She studied at Oxford and London. She has specialized in the working out of new forms of liturgy suited to the needs of families and small groups. She is a member of the Newman Association Family Apostolate Committee. She collaborated with her husband in the writing of *Liturgy is what we make it* (1967), and is co-editor of *Experience of Liturgy* (1968).

ERHARD QUACK was born on 5 January 1904 in Germany and is a Catholic. He studied music, including Church music. He is secretary for Church Music at the Liturgical Institute, Trier, and the author of *Das Kirchenlied in der erneuerten Liturgie* (1969).

HERMAN SCHMIDT, s.j., born 26 June 1912 in The Netherlands, ordained 1940. He studied at Nijmegen, Maastricht, the Pontificio Istituto Orientale, the Pontificio Istituto Musicae Sacrae, and at the Vatican School of Paleography, doctoring in theology in 1946. He has been Professor of Liturgy at the Gregorian since 1947 and at the Pontificio Istituto Liturgico since 1962. His publications include *Liturgie et Langue vulgaire* (1950); *Introductio in Liturgiam Occidentalem* (^{3}1965); and *Constitutie over H. Liturgie* (1964).

ADRIANA ZARRI was born on 26 April 1919 in Italy, and is a Catholic. She studied classics and theology. She is co-editor of the review *Kenosi* and is a committee member of the Associazione Teologica Italiana. Her publications include *Impazienza di Adamo: Ontologia della sessualita* (1964), and *Teologia del probabile* (1967).

International Publishers of CONCILIUM

ENGLISH EDITION
Herder and Herder Inc.
New York, U.S.A.

Burns & Oates Ltd.
London, S.W.1

DUTCH EDITION
Uitgeverij Paul Brand, N.V.
Hilversum, Netherlands

FRENCH EDITION
Maison Mame
Tours/Paris, France

JAPANESE EDITION (PARTIAL)
Nansôsha
Tokyo, Japan

GERMAN EDITION
Verlagsanstalt Benziger & Co., A.G.
Einsiedeln, Switzerland

Matthias Grunewald-Verlag
Mainz, W. Germany

SPANISH EDITION
Ediciones Sigueme
Salamanca, Spain

PORTUGUESE EDITION
Livraria Morais Editoria, Ltda.
Lisbon, Portugal

ITALIAN EDITION
Editrice Queriniana
Brescia, Italy

POLISH EDITION (PARTIAL)
Pallottinum
Poznan-Warsaw, Poland

New theology from Herder and Herder

Leo Scheffczyk
CREATION AND PROVIDENCE
Herder History of Dogma Series

This thoroughly researched study examines the efforts of theologians to reach a deeper understanding of the truth of creation by probing both the ancient sources of revelation and the data of modern biblical science and the scientific method making itself felt within twentieth-century Catholic theology.

$7.95   *February*

Boniface A. Willems
THE REALITY OF REDEMPTION

This timely and groundbreaking theological investigation by the noted Dominican theologian from Holland explores the current indifference to redemption in theology and locates a contemporary meaning for redemption within man's ability to be responsible for his own destiny.

$4.50   *March*

Joseph Ratzinger
INTRODUCTION TO CHRISTIANITY

In this remarkable elucidation, Joseph Ratzinger, scriptural scholar and dogmatic historian, discusses the problem of faith in the modern world in the light of the history, significance and expression of the Creed.

$6.50   *March*

Thomas F. O'Meara
HOLINESS AND RADICALISM
IN RELIGIOUS LIFE

Discussing the crisis in, and future of, religious life with clarity and vision, Fr. O'Meara seeks to discern the catalysts of dramatic change within American religious communities by investigating the factors affecting all of contemporary life: secularization, social change, personhood, and community.

$4.95   *April*

Gabriel Moran
THE NEW COMMUNITY

This exhortation to religious orders to look beyond themselves to the larger society, where both *religion* and *community* are undergoing great changes in form and meaning, is a companion to and extension of the author's *Experiences in Community*. In it he suggests specific changes in existing religious orders to get them moving toward the new religion and the new community and offers a description of the religious community of the future.

$4.50 Cloth; $1.95 Paper   *May*

 DESCLEE

THE GOSPELS AND THE JESUS OF HISTORY
Xavier Leon-Dufour, S. J.

This is a work of massive authority, masterfully written with all the resources of contemporary scholarship. It rises above denominational barriers and tackles the continuously debated question: the historical value of the gospels as a source for an accurate account of Christ. It evaluates all the cogent opinions of the past and the present, from Harnack to Bultmann ... and then submits the texts of the four gospels to an exacting scrutiny. $5.75

Dictionary of BIBLICAL THEOLOGY
Xavier Leon-Dufour, S. J., General Editor

The indispensable work for those who seek an integrated and essential understanding of the Scriptures. Written, for a wide audience, by 70 leading biblical experts—it is edited for quick and reliable reference. "Its scholarship is completely up to date."—*John L. McKenzie, SJ* "This monumental work gives cause for celebration." —*Wilfrid J. Harrington, OP* "Any adult reader who wishes to study the Bible will find it of permanent value."—*The Register* $12.95

THE BIBLE, WORD OF GOD A Theological Introduction to the Study of Scripture
Pierre Grelot

With the pedagogical skill that marks him as one of the finest biblical scholars working today, Pierre Grelot gathers here all that is indispensable for a serious, informed study of Scripture. The book, which is divided into sections on *Sacred Scripture* and *The Interpretation of Scripture,* is a mine of references and detailed treatments of almost all problems raised by the Bible. $9.75

THE NEW LIFE OF GRACE
Piet Fransen

Foreword by Robert Gleason. This thorough biblical and theological study—the standard work in its field —is the crowning accomplishment of a scholar generally regarded as "the theologian of grace." $8.50

 — DESCLEE CO.—

Distributed by
HERDER BOOK CENTER
232 Madison Avenue
New York, N.Y. 10016